Writing Research Papers

2001 Edition

Your complete guide to the process of writing a research paper, from finding a topic to preparing the final manuscript

McDougal Littell
A HOUGHTON MIFFLIN COMPANY

Evanston, Illinois ■ Boston ■ Dallas

Special thanks to Ann Gallagher and Maureen Kelly-Burke of Rockport High School for their help in verifying the suitability of these materials for the classroom.

These materials were prepared by **Robert D. Shepherd**, a licensed teacher of English in the states of Massachusetts and New Hampshire; an educational writer, researcher, and consultant; and a senior partner in Wordworks Publishing Services.

With minor exceptions, this book follows the style for documentation set forth in the *MLA Handbook for Writers of Research Papers*. Documentation style for some recent technologies, including online computer services, has been updated.

The editors have made every effort to trace the ownership of the copyrighted materials found in this book. Any information that would lead to finding sources of unacknowledged materials used in the book would be greatly appreciated.

ISBN 0–618–05324–7

Contents

Research as Exploration and Discovery

Research is about satisfying curiosity, about finding something you are interested in, exploring it, and making discoveries. Research is about extending the range of what you know. It is like sailing off the edge of the map into unknown territory. Research is an exciting adventure, but this adventure requires no fancy equipment. All you really need is curiosity, a desire to find out who, what, where, when, why, and how.

Types of Research

There are two major kinds of research, primary and secondary. **Primary research** involves generating new ideas and information on your own. If you take a note pad into the woods, watch the animals there, and take notes on what you see, that is primary research. If you make up a questionnaire and ask people to answer the questions, that is also primary research. Other examples of primary research are

- Conducting an experiment and recording the results

- Searching through documents at a county courthouse to discover your family history

- Interviewing someone about his or her personal experiences

- Reading a novel and taking notes on your personal responses to it

Secondary research involves gathering and analyzing the results of other people's primary research. Suppose, for example, that you want to learn about life in the Cherokee town of Tenasi before the Europeans came to North America. All that you know to begin with is that the name of the town gave us the name of the state Tennessee. To find out more about the topic, you could do secondary research. You could read books and articles written

> **"** Research is about satisfying curiosity, about finding something you are interested in, exploring it, and making discoveries. **"**

1

about Tenasi, or you could interview historians who have done research on the subject. Most of the work that you will do when you write your research paper will probably be secondary research.

Why Do Research Papers?

Research can be fascinating and glamorous. After all, it is the main activity of most writers, reporters, historians, and scientists. However, research can also be a practical, everyday sort of activity, one useful to people with jobs that are less exotic. Restaurant managers do research to find out what their customers might like. Students do research to find out about careers. Whatever you plan to do with your future, knowing how to do research will be of great value to you, and there is no better introduction to doing research than planning and writing a research paper.

2

Understanding the Research Paper

Have you ever written a report that contained information from several sources? If so, you have already produced something like a research paper. A research paper is a written report that presents the results of a purposeful, focused, in-depth study of a specific topic. Its writer chooses a topic, gathers information about the topic from a number of sources, and then presents that information in an organized way.

Writing a research paper will most likely be the most time-consuming and challenging task that you have ever undertaken as a student. However, do not let the size of the task scare you. You will find researching your paper quite easy if you take it one step at a time, following the guidelines in this book.

Research and the Writing Process

Some types of writing, like taking notes in class or jotting down a grocery list, are done at one time. However, most types of writing are done over a period of time. In other words, writing is a process, and it can be roughly divided into stages—prewriting, drafting, revising, proofreading, and publishing. This book will take you through the following activities in the process of writing a research paper.

> **"** Don't let the size of the task scare you. You will find researching your paper quite easy if you take it one step at a time, following the guidelines in this book. **"**

The Research Process

- Choosing your subject
- Doing preliminary research
- Limiting your subject to a specific topic

> " Writing is a process, and it can be roughly divided into stages—prewriting, drafting, revising, proofreading, and publishing. "

The Research Process (cont.)

- Finding an angle and writing a statement of controlling purpose

- Preparing a list of possible sources (a working bibliography)

- Taking notes and developing a rough, or working, outline

- Organizing your notes and making a final outline

- Writing your first draft

- Revising your draft

- Writing the final draft, with a complete Works Cited list

As you work through the next few chapters, you will come to understand more clearly what constitutes a successful research paper. For now, read the sample research paper on the following pages. Then answer the questions at the end of the paper.

Mother and two children on road at Tule Lake, California, September, 1939. Photo by Dorothea Lange, courtesy of the Library of Congress.

Maika Carlos-Díaz

Ms. Lee

Junior English

15 October 1999

The Political Message of John Steinbeck's

<u>The Grapes of Wrath</u>

A novel, like a movie, is a form of entertainment. However, some novels do a great deal more than entertain. Some pack a powerful political message. For example, <u>Uncle Tom's Cabin</u>, by Harriet Beecher Stowe, created controversy from the moment it was published. <u>The Jungle</u>, by Upton Sinclair, alerted the country to the horrors of the meatpacking industry.

John Steinbeck's <u>The Grapes of Wrath</u> is another example of a novel with a powerful political message. It warned that exploitation of migrant workers would cause them to rise up as a group against their oppressors, the state and the wealthy landowners. But beyond that, the novel shows how such an oppressive situation can result in a profound philosophical change in the people who experience it.

The following pages examine the political and philosophical message in Steinbeck's novel. First, they explain the historical and economic situation to which Steinbeck was reacting. Then they present Steinbeck's opinions about that situation. Finally, they show how the events in the novel reflect Steinbeck's beliefs about both the political and the human changes that can result from continued oppression.

<u>The Grapes of Wrath</u> is a historical novel, "a summation of national experience at a given time" (Levant 93). Therefore, to understand the novel, one must understand the historical events on which it was based. The historical and economic experience that Steinbeck was reacting to was that of the

First paragraph presents some background information to provide a context for the thesis statement.

Thesis statement

This paragraph helps the reader to get his or her bearings by outlining the argument to be presented in the rest of the paper.

Titles of long works are underlined.

This is the standard form for parenthetical documentation. The author's last name is followed by the page number or numbers.

The writer uses a combination of quotations, paraphrases, and summaries to support her points.

migrants who left the Oklahoma Dust Bowl in the late 1930s ("Dust Bowl"). In Oklahoma, storms blew away topsoil (Frazier 204), covered pastures, and suffocated livestock (Tannehill 7). At the time, the country was in the grip of a severe economic downturn called the Great Depression ("Great Depression"). Crop failure, added to already low crop prices, "led to the foreclosure of many small farms and the subsequent homelessness of many farm families" (Frazier 204).

The first section of this paper, the part that tells about the historical background of the novel, is arranged chronologically (in time order).

Between 300,000 and 400,000 homeless farmers from the Dust Bowl area packed their possessions into old cars or trucks and headed to California to find work (Stein 216). The panhandle region of Oklahoma and Texas lost more than half its residents. However, when these people got to California, they did not find the paradise they were looking for. They found "not a Promised Land but a man-blighted Eden" (Crockett 195). As one Oklahoma refugee put it in a song,

Indent a quotation of more than four lines ten spaces from the left margin. Leave two character spaces at the end of the quotation. Then give the parenthetical citation.

> Lots of folks back East, they say, leavin' home every
>   day.
> Beatin' that hot, ole, dusty way to the California
>   line.
> 'Cross the desert sands they roll, gettin' out of the
>   ole Dust Bowl,
> Thinkin' they're goin' to a sugar bowl, but here is
>   what they find:

The line of dots shows that one or more complete lines has been left out in the quotation from a poem or, in this case, a song.

> [. . . . .]
> California's a Garden of Eden, a paradise to live in
>   or see,
> But believe it or not, you won't find it so hot,
> If you ain't got the Do-Re-Me. (Guthrie)

Most of the migrants who arrived in California didn't have any "Do-Re-Me," or money. When they arrived, they camped out and looked for work in California's fruit and cotton fields (Stein 210).

These immigrants discovered that California agriculture was based on enormous farms, or "factories in the field" (McWilliams 42). These farms were "cultivated by migratory laborers who miraculously turned up for the harvest and disappeared once the crops were laid by" (Stein 205).

The immigrants from Oklahoma swelled the numbers of California's migrant labor force and drove wages down (Stein 213-24). Wages were so low, and jobs were so few, that thousands of migrants were driven to desperate poverty. The extent of the desperation is made clear in a report written in 1939, the year that The Grapes of Wrath was published:

> The State Relief Administration estimates that most agricultural workers only have employment for six months in the year or less; and that the average yearly earnings per family [. . . were] $289 in 1935. In the same study the S.R.A. estimated that each family [. . .] should have had at least $780 to eke out an existence. [. . .]In 1932 there were 181 agricultural workers for every 100 jobs offered; in [. . .] 1934, 142.(McWilliams 48)

In other words, the migrant workers were attempting to live on less than half what they needed just to survive, there were far more workers than there were jobs, and what few jobs there were disappeared entirely for half of each year.

Unable to find work, scorned and hounded from place to place, the migrants from Oklahoma gathered together in settlements along highways, places that became known as Hoovervilles, after President Herbert Hoover. An actress who visited one of these camps wrote, "I went around in a sick daze for hours after witnessing unimaginable suffering" (qtd.

No paragraph indention is necessary if the quoted material is one paragraph or less.

The brackets around the ellipsis points indicate that the points do not appear in the source being quoted. They have been included by the paper's writer to show that words in the source have been omitted here.

7

in Stein 219). These settlements were full of hunger and
disease. According to historian Walter Stein, "By 1937, the
[Oklahoma migrants] had become a local embarrassment, by 1938
a state concern, and by 1939, with the publication of <u>The
Grapes of Wrath</u>, a national scandal" (216).

> If the name of the author of the source is given in the text of the paper, then the citation need include only the page number.

Steinbeck's reaction to the migrants and their situation
paralleled the comments of the actress who visited the camp.
However, despite being angered and disturbed by the migrants'
plight, Steinbeck was reluctant to write about it. When <u>Life</u>
magazine asked him to write about the migrants, he declined,
saying that he didn't want to profit from the migrants' misery.
Later, though, Steinbeck wrote a series of newspaper articles
to draw attention to the migrants' problems. Steinbeck
actually followed the trail of the Oklahoma migrants and
visited their camping places (French, "What Did" 51-52). He
also made friends with Tom Collins, who ran a federal relief
camp for the migrants. From Collins, he learned as much as he
could about the migrants' lives (Demott xxvii-xxviii).
Steinbeck later told an interviewer, "I know what I was
talking about [in <u>The Grapes of Wrath</u>]. I lived, off and on,
with those [migrants] for [. . .] three years" (Cameron 19).

> This paragraph begins the second section of the paper, which discusses Steinbeck's reactions to the migrant situation.
>
> Generally speaking, each major section of a research paper should begin with such a transitional paragraph, one that presents the main idea of the section.

> Brackets can be used to add necessary information to a quotation, but make sure that the added material does not change the meaning of the quotation.

In 1938, the year before he published <u>The Grapes of
Wrath</u>, Steinbeck wrote a nonfiction pamphlet about the
migrants. This pamphlet made Steinbeck's opinions about the
migrant situation very clear. Entitled <u>Their Blood Is Strong</u>,
the pamphlet told about the horrible conditions of the
migrants' lives. Steinbeck wrote in the pamphlet that the
migrants' camps were full of sickness--of pneumonia, measles,
tuberculosis, rickets, and pellagra (89). The migrants also
faced an even more terrible problem:

8

> There has been no war in California, no plague, no
> bombing of open towns and roads, no shelling of
> cities. It is a beautiful year. And thousands of
> families are starving. [. . .]
>
>   [It's] in the tents you see along the roads and
>   in the shacks built from dump heap materials that the
>   hunger is, and it isn't malnutrition. It is
>   starvation. (88)

In his pamphlet, Steinbeck went beyond describing
existing conditions. He also warned that terrible anger was
building among the migrants:

> Dignity is all gone, and [their] spirit has turned to
> sullen anger. [. . .] We regard this destruction of
> dignity [. . .] as one of the most regrettable
> results of the migrant's life, since it does [. . .]
> make [of the migrant] a sullen outcast who will
> strike at our government in any way that occurs to
> him. (62, 70)

Steinbeck repeated this warning several times in the
pamphlet. He wrote, for example, that the mistreatment of the
migrants "constitutes a criminal endangering of the peace of
the state" (69). In another place in the pamphlet he said that
California "is gradually building a human structure [migrant
labor] which will certainly change the state, and may [. . .]
destroy the present system of agricultural economics" (59). So
it was Steinbeck's opinion that the migrant situation was
explosive and might lead to insurrection against the
government.

The Grapes of Wrath elaborates on and puts into story
form the political warning that Steinbeck made in his pamphlet
Their Blood Is Strong. In the novel Steinbeck shows how
oppression inevitably turns nonpolitical people into political

When quoting more than one paragraph, indent all full paragraphs in the quotation an additional three spaces.

Both the author and the title of the source of this quotation are mentioned in the text, so all that is needed is the page number.

When quoted material appears in the source on nonconsecutive pages, give the first page number, a comma, and then the number of the page on which the material is continued.

This paragraph introduces the third section of the paper, which discusses the political message of the novel.

people. It drives them to join with others who are oppressed. When that happens, a group emerges, and a group is a potentially potent force. But the novel also elaborates on this change by showing that it is accompanied by a philosophical shift from a self-centered focus on the individual to a focus on people as a community.

The novel shows the political and philosophical evolution of the migrants through the story of a single migrant family, the Joads. At the beginning of the novel, the Joads, like most of the displaced farmers of that era, see themselves as helpless victims of natural and economic events beyond their control. They feel powerless to fight against the system that is running people off their land. One tenant farmer, searching for someone to blame for the loss of his farm, considers blaming the tractor driver who is knocking his house down. But the tractor driver is just taking orders from the bank. The bank has a president and a board of directors, but they are just taking orders from the East. The people in the East are just responding to economic events. No one is really responsible or in charge (49; ch. 5). In this early historical chapter, Steinbeck is setting the stage for the seemingly overwhelming odds that the Joads must face.

Having lost their land, the Joads look for a simple solution that will make everything all right. They have seen handbills from California, promising lots of work and high wages (117; ch. 10). California therefore becomes the promised land. Ma Joad dreams of getting a little white house in California, surrounded by orange trees (118; ch. 10). Grampa Joad dreams of picking "a wash tub full of grapes" and sitting down in it (119; ch. 10). The family sees California as a kind of paradise, and the symbol of this paradise is its fruit (Crockett 195). At this point the Joads have still not taken

When referring to a passage of a literary work that is available in different editions or from different publishers, give the line numbers (for short works) or chapter numbers (for long works like novels) or act, scene, and line numbers (for plays). The reader of the paper can then find the passage no matter what edition he or she is using.

responsibility for improving their situation. Instead, they simply set out for an Eden.

However, paradise turns out not to be so easily attainable. Steinbeck shows how on their arrival in California the Joads, and others like them, can begin a change from a naive, resigned unit to a thoughtful, questioning group of individuals. In California the Joads meet a father and a son who warn them that California is not a paradise. The father points out that the land is all owned by large companies. People go hungry while land lies fallow, or unworked, because "ever'thing in California is owned" (264-65; ch. 18). This is the first stage of the Joads' political education. However, the Joads have no choice but to ignore the warning and go on.

In Hooverville, a roadside migrant settlement that the Joads pass through, Steinbeck shows the migrants' dawning anger and their first hesitant steps toward rebellion. A young man named Floyd explains to Tom the foolhardiness of coming to California on the strength of a handbill advertising work. Floyd explains that the wealthy landowners in California send out thousands of handbills to attract a surplus of crop pickers. The workers then compete with one another and drive wages down. Tom suggests to Floyd the possibility of organized resistance:

> Tom said angrily, "Them peaches got to be picked right now, don't they? Jus' when they're ripe?"
>
> "'Course they do."
>
> "Well, s'pose them people got together an' says, 'Let 'em rot.' Wouldn' be long 'fore the price went up, by God!"

However, Floyd points out that whenever anyone tries to become a leader, he is simply jailed or killed, and his family also suffers (315-17; ch. 20).

But despite the warning, Tom Joad has begun to change. In the beginning of the novel, he is portrayed as someone concerned only with himself and his own immediate affairs. Statements such as "I'm jus' puttin' one foot in front a the other" and "I climb fences when I got fences to climb" demonstrate this point (223-24; ch. 16). However, in Hooverville Tom risks his own neck to protect Floyd from a deputy. By sticking one foot in front of the deputy and tripping him when the deputy is about to arrest Floyd for being a "red," Tom begins his transformation into a political and involved person (339-40; ch. 20). For the first time, Tom takes an active role and sees the need to reach out and help another person.

Tom's mother, too, starts to think politically, and beyond herself. As the Joads leave Hooverville, they are confronted by an angry mob of locals who have come to burn down the camp. Tom evades them, and Ma says defiantly, "They ain't gonna wipe us out. [. . .] A different time's comin'" (360; ch. 20). Through these two characters, Steinbeck is showing that the passive, helpless migrants of the Dust Bowl evolve as thinking individuals as they assess their life experiences.

The Joads' next stop is Weedpatch, a government camp for migrants. There Steinbeck presents the idea that the migrants can learn that good things are indeed possible if people work together for a common cause. At Weedpatch there are no policemen. The people live together in dignity. Timothy Wallace, a migrant at the camp who helps Tom find a job, describes Weedpatch in this way:

> This here camp is a organization. People there look
> out for theirselves. Got the nicest strang band in
> these parts. Got a little charge account in the store
> for folks that's hungry. Fi' dollars--you can git
> that much food an' the camp'll stan' good. We ain't
> never had no trouble with the law. I guess the big
> farmers is scairt of that. Can't throw us in jail--
> why, it scares 'em. Figger maybe if we can gove'n
> ourselves, maybe we'll do other things. (382; ch. 22)

Tom and other men in the camp successfully organize to
stop a plan to cause a riot at Weedpatch. Through Weedpatch
the Joads learn that the concept of organized resistance, first
introduced at Hooverville, can be successfully executed for
the good of the community. Pa Joad points out, "They's change
a-comin'. I don' know what. Maybe we won't live to see her.
But she's a-comin'. They's a res'less feelin'" (443; ch. 24).

Outside the peace of Weedpatch, however, a corrupt system
is still feeding the migrants' anger. In order for the
agricultural associations to keep food prices high, the excess
fruit is destroyed or goes to waste. Steinbeck's account of
sickness in migrant camps in Their Blood Is Strong seems to
echo in the fruit imagery:

> Carloads of oranges dumped on the ground. [. . .] A
> million people hungry, needing the fruit. [. . .]
> And the smell of rot fills the country. [. . .] And
> children dying of pellagra must die because a profit
> cannot be taken from an orange. And coroners must
> fill in the certificates--died of malnutrition--
> because the food must rot, must be forced to rot.
> (448-49; ch. 25)

13

Steinbeck makes the effect of this waste on the migrants clear: "[I]n the eyes of the hungry there is a growing wrath. In the souls of the people the grapes of wrath are filling and growing heavy, growing heavy for the vintage" (449; ch. 25).

Steinbeck's reference to wrath points to the significance of the title, The Grapes of Wrath, which in turn shows his belief in the transforming power of the migrants' anger. The immediate source of the title is the first stanza of "The Battle Hymn of the Republic," a song of the Civil War era by Julia Ward Howe:

> Mine eyes have seen the glory of the coming of the
>> Lord;
> He is trampling out the vintage where the
>> grapes of wrath are stored [. . .]
> (Familiar Quotations 566)

Steinbeck's novel is also a battle hymn, but one about the issue of migrant labor rather than the issue of slavery. In addition to Howe's song, there is another source for Steinbeck's title. In the Bible, the Revelation of St. John mentions "the wine of wrath" forced upon people by a "Babylon" that is "fallen" (Rev. 14.8; Crockett 195). Babylon was an ancient city-state described in the Bible as a wicked place. In his title Steinbeck seems to be suggesting that the migrants, having learned to think of themselves as part of a group, might draw upon their anger and rise up to overthrow the Babylon, or state, that has mistreated them so horribly. The wine of their wrath will cause Babylon to fall. That's just what Steinbeck had predicted in his pamphlet Their Blood Is Strong.

Contrasting with Weedpatch is another of the Joads' stops--the Pixley camp, a place run by the Hooper ranch, a large agricultural concern. Conditions are terrible, and when

14

the pay drops to 2.5 cents a day, the Joads face real hunger (491; ch. 26). In Pixley, the owners of the camp employ armed guards who patrol the place, including the movement of its residents (473-74; ch. 26).

The climactic event of the novel occurs when Tom's friend Casy, who has actively tried to organize resistance to the system, is killed by a deputy. Tom kills the deputy and is forced into hiding (495-99; ch. 26). He has now risked everything and sees the full potential of organized resistance. As Tom says to his mother, "I been a-wonderin' why we can't do that all over. Throw out the cops that ain't our people. All work together for our own thing [. . .]" (536; ch. 28). Tom then commits himself to working, as Casy did, as a labor organizer.

Similarly, the men around him are changing. Steinbeck extends his theme of change and transformation by showing migrants gathering together and turning their mistreatment into anger:

> The women watched the men, watched to see whether the break had come at last. The women stood silently and watched. And where a number of men gathered together, the fear went from their faces, and anger took its place. And the women sighed with relief, for they knew it was all right--the break had not come; and the break would never come as long as fear could turn to wrath.
>
> Tiny points of grass came through the earth, and in a few days the hills were pale green with the beginning year. (556; ch. 29)

Springtime and green grass are traditional symbols of rebirth and renewal. This passage seems to suggest that when the migrants gather as a group, they become angry. This

15

gathering signals the beginning of a new world for them, and perhaps an end to the world of their oppressors.

The change in the migrants goes beyond a purely political one, however. They have also learned to reach out to one another, to become one family. For example, when Tom decides to become a labor organizer, he no longer worries about himself and his own affairs. In fact, when Ma wonders aloud whether Tom might be killed as a result of his organizing activities, he replies:

> "Well, maybe like Casy says, a fella ain't got a soul of his own, but on'y a piece of a big one--an' then----"

> "Then what, Tom?"

> "Then it don' matter. Then I'll be all aroun' in the dark. I'll be ever'where--wherever you look. Wherever they's a fight so hungry people can eat, I'll be there. Wherever they's a cop beatin' up a guy, I'll be there. If Casy knowed, why, I'll be in the way guys yell when they're mad an'--I'll be in the way kids laugh when they're hungry an' they know supper's ready. An' when our folks eat the stuff they raise an' live in the houses they build--why, I'll be there. See?" (537; ch. 28)

Tom has learned to think of himself as part of a larger group of oppressed people like himself. His own welfare and the welfare of the group have merged.

Ma also has gone through a transformation. In the early part of the novel, Ma is concerned only with her immediate family. For instance, during the family's trip to California, she says, "All we got is the family unbroke" (219; ch. 16). In other words, people beyond the family can't be counted on. Near the end of the novel, though, Ma shows how completely she has changed her point of view. She says directly that the family used to be her primary concern but that now she cares about people in general: "Use' ta be the fambly was fust. It ain't so now. It's anybody. Worse off we get, the more we got to do" (569; ch. 30).

Ma, like her son Tom, has learned to see herself not as an isolated person or as a member of an isolated family but rather as a member of the human family. And this, Steinbeck seems to imply, is the power of the people. Their resistance has become not just a political cause, but a powerful moral one as well.

The Grapes of Wrath presents in story form Steinbeck's reading of the migrant situation. In his novel Steinbeck warns about the explosiveness of the migrant situation by showing how members of one migrant family become politicized. In the conclusion of his novel and in its title, Steinbeck suggests that the migrants have become a cohesive group driven by anger.

By showing how the Joads come to worry about people other than themselves, Steinbeck is showing, as he did in Their Blood Is Strong, that the mistreatment of the migrants will bind them together into a politically powerful group. That group, Steinbeck affirms, may threaten the government and the economic system that has oppressed them, but the threat is based on an unshakable sense of community and morality. As Ma suggests in the novel and in the conclusion of the film version of The Grapes of Wrath, the human spirit is unbreakable: "We'll go on forever. [. . .]We're the people."

The conclusion of the paper is presented in two paragraphs. The writer begins her conclusion by restating her thesis in different words.

Works Cited

Newspaper article reprinted in another source
Cameron, Tom. "<u>The Grapes of Wrath</u> Author Guards Self from Threats at Moody Gulch." <u>Los Angeles Times</u> 9 July 1939: 1-2. Rpt. in <u>Conversations with John Steinbeck</u>. Ed. Thomas Fensch. Jackson: UP of Mississippi, 1988. 19-20.

Journal article
Crockett, H. Kelly. "The Bible and <u>The Grapes of Wrath</u>." <u>College English</u> 24 (1962): 193-99.

Introduction to a book edited by the writer of the introduction
Demott, Robert. Introduction. <u>Working Days: The Journals of</u> The Grapes of Wrath: <u>1938-1941</u>. Ed. Demott. New York: Viking-Penguin, 1989. xxi-lvii.

Online information service
"Dust Bowl." <u>Compton's Encyclopedia Online</u>. Vers.3.0.1998. America Online. 50 ct. 1999. Keyword: Compton's.

Collection (The same work could be listed by editor or compiler if you wish to emphasize that information.)
<u>Familiar Quotations: A Collection of Passages, Phrases and Proverbs Traced to Their Sources in Ancient and Modern Literature</u>. Comp. John Bartlett. Ed. Emily Morrison Beck. 15th ed. Boston: Little, 1980. 566.

Frazier, Thomas R., ed. <u>Since 1865</u>. 2nd ed. New York: Harcourt, 1978. Vol. 2 of <u>The Underside of American History: Other Readings</u>. 2 vols. 1971-78.

French, Warren, ed. <u>A Companion to</u> The Grapes of Wrath. New York: Viking, 1963.

Three hyphens used to indicate another work by the same person
---."What Did John Steinbeck Know About the 'Okies'?" French, <u>Companion</u> 51-53.

Movie
<u>The Grapes of Wrath</u>. Screenplay by Nunnally Johnson. Dir. John Ford. Perf. John Carradine, Jane Darwell, and Henry Fonda. Twentieth Century-Fox, 1940.

Article in reference database
"Great Depression." <u>Encyclopaedia Britannica Online</u>. Vers.99.1. Encyclopaedia Britannica. 5 Oct. 1999 <http://www.eb.com:180/bol/topic? ev=38610&sctn=1#s-top>.

Recording
Guthrie, Woody. "Do-Re-Me." <u>Dust Bowl Ballads</u>. Rounder, 1988.

Levant, Howard. "The Fully Matured Art: <u>The Grapes of Wrath</u>."

<u>The Novels of John Steinbeck: A Critical Study</u>. Columbia:

U of Missouri P, 1974. 93-129.

McWilliams, Carey. "The End of a Cycle." <u>Factories in the</u>

<u>Field</u>. Boston: Little, 1939. 305-25. Rpt. in French,

<u>Companion</u> 42-49.

Stein, Walter J. "The Okie Impact." <u>California and the Dust</u>

<u>Bowl Migration</u>. Westport: Greenwood, 1973. 32-64. Rpt. in

Frazier, 205-34.

Steinbeck, John. <u>The Grapes of Wrath</u>. 1939. New York:

Penguin, 1999.

---.<u>Their Blood Is Strong</u>. San Francisco: Lubin, 1938.

Rpt. in French, <u>Companion</u> 53-92.

Tannehill, Ivan Ray. "Dusters and Black Blizzards." <u>Drought:</u>

<u>Its Causes and Effects</u>. Princeton: Princeton UP, 1948.

10-12, 44-51. Rpt. in French, <u>Companion</u> 5-8.

Work in a collection

Republished work (Note that the date of first publication is given after the title.)

Migrant woman and children. Photo by Dorothea Lange, courtesy of the Library of Congress.

Think and Respond

In your learning log, in your writing folder, or in a group discussion, analyze the sample research paper on the previous pages. Respond to these questions about the paper:

1. What information appears in the heading of the paper? at the top of each page?

2. What is the main idea, or thesis, of the paper? Does the writer support her thesis? How?

3. What are the major parts of the body of the paper? What is the main point in each part? Does the order of the parts make sense? Why or why not?

4. How does the writer of the paper indicate, within the paper, that she has taken material from a source?

5. Where does the writer's complete list of sources appear, and what is it called?

6. Does the writer use a wide variety of sources? What different kinds of sources does she use?

7. How does the writer introduce her paper?

8. How does the writer conclude her paper?

9. Does the writer use evidence skillfully to support the claims that she makes? Give two examples.

10. What suggestions for improvement might you give this writer if you had a chance to do so?

Migrants camped by a roadside. Photo by Dorothea Lange, courtesy of the Library of Congress.

Discovering a Topic for Research

2

O ne of the most important parts of doing a research paper is choosing a topic. By choosing wisely, you can ensure that your research will go smoothly and that you will enjoy doing it.

Choosing a Subject That You Care About

A **subject** is a broad area of interest, such as African-American history or astronomy or sports. One way to approach the search for a research-paper topic is first to choose a general area of interest and then to focus on some part of it. Make sure that you have a real reason for wanting to explore the subject. Often the best subjects for research papers are ones that are related to your own life or to the lives of people you know.

If you are already keeping a "writing ideas" list in your journal or in your writing portfolio, you can refer to that list for possible subjects. If you are not regularly listing your writing ideas, you might consider starting to do so now.

You can begin exploring general subject areas that interest you by completing the following interest inventory.

" Often the best subjects for research papers are ones that are directly related to your own life or to the lives of people you know. **"**

Interest Inventory

Respond in writing to the following questions:

1. What activities do I enjoy?

2. What subjects do I enjoy reading about?

3. What books have I enjoyed reading in the past?

Interest Inventory (cont.)

4. What subjects have captured my attention and interest in my classes?

5. What questions do I really want to know the answers to? (Write six questions, beginning with the words *who, what, where, when, why,* and *how.*)

6. What commonplace things are complete mysteries to me? What ordinary things—such as a sunset, a nuclear reactor, a computer hard drive, a human heart, flight, or diving gear—would I like to understand more completely?

7. What interesting careers or hobbies do my friends, acquaintances, or relatives have? What interesting experiences have they had?

8. If I could have a long conversation with someone from any place and from any time in history, who would that person be?

If your answers to the interest-inventory questions don't suggest a general subject area that you would like to learn more about, try the following activities.

Searching for a Subject

1. Spend some time in a library, simply walking up and down the aisles or browsing through the card catalog, looking for subjects that appeal to you.

2. Browse through encyclopedias, almanacs, atlases, dictionaries, or recent periodical indexes. Useful indexes include the *Readers' Guide to Periodical Literature* and the *Humanities Index.*

Searching for a Subject (cont.)

3. Glance at the tables of contents in your textbooks, looking for subjects that you'd like to know more about.

4. If you have access to an electronic encyclopedia, a knowledge database, or a computer index that covers general subjects, start with an interesting search word, see where that leads, and try the subheadings or cross-references that come up.

5. Watch some public-television specials that deal with nature, with science, with travel, with history, or with the future, or listen to some public-radio programs that deal with these matters. See if any of the subjects of the programs capture your imagination.

6. Look through newsmagazines for subjects related to current events.

7. List some novels or stories that you have read recently, and think about possible subjects related to these. Look through your literature textbook for other possibilities.

> "Spend some time in a library, simply walking up and down the aisles or browsing through the card catalog, looking for subjects that appeal to you."

Limiting Your Subject/Choosing a Topic

Once you have a **general subject** that you are interested in, such as migrant workers or animal communication, the next step is to narrow that subject to a **specific topic** that can be treated in a research paper.

Doing Preliminary Research

If you already know a great deal about your subject, then you can probably think of a specific topic to research in that subject area. However, if you are not already an expert, it is a good idea to do some preliminary research to identify potential topics. Here are a few suggestions for preliminary research.

Ideas for Preliminary Research

- Read encyclopedia articles and relevant Web sites.

- List questions about the subject, and interview someone knowledgeable about it.

- Brainstorm with friends, classmates, or relatives to find out what they know about the subject.

- Check the *Readers' Guide to Periodical Literature* to find general articles on your subject.

- Find a textbook that covers the general field of study to which your subject belongs. Read about your subject in that textbook.

- Go to the place in the library where books on the subject are shelved. Choose books at random and look them over.

Here is how one student conducted her preliminary research.

One Student's Process: Maika

When Maika was completing her interest inventory, she paused at the question about interesting experiences that relatives have had. Maika's grandfather came from Guatemala by way of Mexico. As a young man, he had been a migrant worker. Surely there were many aspects of her grandfather's experiences or of the culture of his native land that would make interesting topics for a research paper. Maika decided to interview her grandfather about his early experiences.

Using Prewriting Techniques

In addition to conducting preliminary research, you may also be able to come up with a specific topic by using one of the following prewriting techniques:

1. **Freewriting or clustering.** Write whatever comes to mind about the subject for five minutes, or draw a cluster diagram in which you use lines to connect your topic with related ideas.

2. **Brainstorming.** Working with a group of friends or classmates, write down a list of topics that come to mind as people think about the subject.

3. **Questioning.** Write a list of questions about the subject. Begin each question with the word *who, what, where, when, why,* or *how,* or start your questions with *What if . . .*

4. **Discussion.** Listen to what other students know about your subject, what aspects of it they find intriguing, and what difficulties they think you might have in researching it.

Evaluating Possible Topics

Once you have generated a list of ideas for possible topics, you need to evaluate them. That is, you need to judge them on the basis of certain criteria. Here are some criteria for judging a research topic:

1. **The topic should be interesting.** Often the most interesting topic is one that is related to your family's history, to your future, to your major goals, to the place where you live or would like to live, to a career that interests you, or to a hobby or other activity that you enjoy. The topic might be something that has caught your interest in the past, perhaps something you have read about or have studied in school.

2. **The topic should be covered in readily available sources.** When considering a topic, always check the catalogs of a few local libraries and the *Readers' Guide to Periodical Literature* to see if sources are available.

> "The topic might be something that has caught your interest in the past, perhaps something you have read about or have studied in school."

3. The topic should be significant. Choose a topic that is significant for you, one worth your time and energy.

4. The topic should be objective. Make sure that your topic is one that can be supported with facts.

5. The topic should not involve simply repeating material available in other sources. Look for a topic that allows you to come up with your own angle or approach.

6. The topic should be narrow enough to be treated fully. Ask your teacher how many pages long your paper should be, and choose a topic that is narrow enough to be treated in a paper of that length.

Writing a Statement of Controlling Purpose

Once you have decided on a specific topic, your next step is to write a **statement of controlling purpose.** This is a sentence or pair of sentences that tells what you want to accomplish in your paper. It is called a statement of controlling purpose because it controls, or guides, your research. The statement of controlling purpose usually contains one or more keywords that tell what the paper is going to accomplish. Keywords that often appear in statements of controlling purpose include *analyze, classify, compare, contrast, define, describe, determine, establish, explain, identify, prove,* and *support.*

Here are two examples of statements of controlling purpose:

> The purpose of this paper is to describe the elements that give the prose writing of Sandra Cisneros a poetic quality.

> The purpose of this paper is to contrast animal communication and human language to show how they are different.

To come up with a statement of controlling purpose, you will probably have to do a considerable amount of preliminary research. That is because before you can write a statement of controlling purpose, you have to know enough about your topic to have a general idea of what you want to say in your paper. Here is an example of one student's process.

Maika's grandfather had been a migrant worker when he first came to California from Guatemala. Maika was interested in learning more about the migrant experience, so she asked her teacher if she knew of any interesting books on the subject. Her teacher recommended John Steinbeck's *The Grapes of Wrath*. Maika read the novel. Then she went to the library and looked up Steinbeck and *The Grapes of Wrath* in the catalog. She found several collections of critical essays about the novel. As she looked through these essays, she found that several subjects were discussed over and over. She made a list of these subjects:

Steinbeck's characterizations of women

Biblical symbolism in *The Grapes of Wrath*

Steinbeck's theory that people in groups have exceptional powers

The Grapes of Wrath as a political novel

She decided that she would write a paper that would explain the political message of Steinbeck's novel. Her statement of controlling purpose was "The purpose of this paper is to explain the political message of John Steinbeck's *The Grapes of Wrath*."

> " To come up with a statement of controlling purpose, you will probably have to do a considerable amount of preliminary research. "

Here are some examples of types of controlling purpose.

Statements of Controlling Purpose

A controlling purpose can be to . . .

Support (or argue against) a policy: The purpose of this paper is to persuade people that foreign-language instruction should begin in elementary school.

Prove (or disprove) one or more statements of fact: The purpose of this paper is to prove that tobacco is a harmful and addictive drug.

Determine the relative values of two or more things: The purpose of this paper is to compare solar, wind, and wave energy to determine which is the most reliable, practical, and cost-effective alternative energy source.

Analyze something into its parts and show how the parts relate to one another: The purpose of this paper is to describe the stages in the television production process and to explain how those stages are interrelated.

Define something: The purpose of this paper is to define the phrase *freedom of the press* by explaining the nature of and limits on press freedom under the law.

Explain causes or effects: The purpose of this paper is to explain the various causes of the destruction of Brazil's rain forests.

Establish a cause-effect relationship: The purpose of this paper is to present the scientific evidence that suggests that cigarette smoking causes cancer.

Describe the development of something over time: The purpose of this paper is to describe how rock 'n' roll developed from blues, gospel, and country music.

Identify and describe a general trend: The purpose of this paper is to show that a major extinction of South American plant and animal species is now occurring.

Classify individual items into groups or categories: The purpose of this paper is to classify African myths into several distinct categories, such as creation stories and lineage stories.

Relate a part to a whole: The purpose of this paper is to examine the place of earthworms in the ecosystem of a forest.

Compare or contrast two subjects to show how they are similar or different: The purpose of this paper is to compare and contrast the views of nature in the poetry of Emily Dickinson and Robert Frost.

Examine a technique: The purpose of this paper is to examine the use of allegory in *The Scarlet Letter,* by Nathaniel Hawthorne.

Explain a general concept by means of specific examples: The purpose of this paper is to explain the concept of paradox by means of examples from math, language, and art.

Explain the main idea or message of something: The purpose of this paper is to explain the political message of John Steinbeck's *The Grapes of Wrath.*

This list of types of controlling purpose is far from complete, so do not worry if the controlling purpose that you come up with does not fall into one of the categories on the list. Do bear in mind that your controlling purpose should be one that is significant to you and, potentially, to your readers.

Bear in mind, as well, that your controlling purpose may change as you do your research. When you begin writing your research paper, you will replace your statement of controlling purpose with a **thesis statement,** a statement of your main idea. The thesis statement will not contain the phrase "the purpose of this paper is." For more information on writing thesis statements, see pages 53–54.

Finding and Recording Your Sources

O nce you have written a statement of controlling purpose, you are ready to put together a list of potential sources. This list of sources that might be useful to you in writing your paper is called a **working bibliography.** You will already have used some sources during your preliminary research, and you will probably want to include some or all of those sources in your working bibliography. As you continue to research and draft, you may discover that some of the sources in your initial list are not useful, and you will undoubtedly find new sources to add to the list. Before you decide to add any source to your list, however, be sure to evaluate it. Information on how to evaluate a source can be found on pages 31–32.

Both print and nonprint sources will be available to you, and you will want to take advantage of both. Here are some good places to start looking for information:

1. Other people. People can be a researcher's greatest resource. Consider interviewing a professor at a local college or university or people who work for businesses, museums, historical societies, or other organizations.

2. Institutions and organizations. Museums, art galleries, dance studios, performing arts centers, schools for the arts, historical societies, and businesses are good sources of information about some topics.

3. The government. Many libraries have special departments that contain government publications. For some topics, you may want to contact town, city, county, state, or federal government offices directly. Listings of government departments and agencies can be found in telephone directories.

4. The library/media center. Remember that a library is more than just a place for housing books. Libraries also contain periodicals—such as newspapers, magazines, and journals—and

" People can be a researcher's greatest resource. "

most have many nonprint materials, such as audio recordings, videotapes, CD-ROM, computer software, reproductions of artworks, and pamphlets.

5. Bookstores. For some topics, the latest information can be found at your local bookstore. If you do not find what you are looking for, ask a bookstore employee to look up your subject or author in *Books in Print.*

6. Bibliographies. A **bibliography** is a list of books and other materials about a particular topic. Your reference librarian can point you to general bibliographies dealing with many subjects such as chemistry, the humanities, or plays by Shakespeare. You can also look for bibliographic lists in the backs of books about your topic.

7. Online information services. An **online information service,** or **computer information service,** is an information source that can be communicated with by means of a personal computer and a modem. For information about online computer services, see Appendix A on pages 77–78.

8. Reference works. Reference works include almanacs, atlases, bibliographies, dictionaries, encyclopedias, periodical indexes, and thesauri. You will find these and similar works in the reference department of your library.

9. Other sources. Do not neglect television programs, live theater performances, radio shows, recordings, videotapes, computer software, and other possible sources of information. Many libraries have extensive collections of audiovisual materials of all kinds, on a wide variety of subjects. Make use of these.

Evaluating Possible Sources

After you locate a potential source, you need to decide whether it will be useful to you. The following questions will help you to evaluate a source:

1. Is the source authoritative? An **authoritative source** is one that can be relied upon to provide accurate information. Consider the reputation of the publication and of the author. Are they well respected?

Research Tip

History and Social Studies

Local government offices can often be useful to people who are doing historical research. For example, a county court clerk's office might be able to help you find copies of deeds, birth records, marriage records, and other documents.

2. Is the source unbiased? An **unbiased source** is one whose author lacks any prejudices that would make his or her work unreliable. For example, a newsletter article claiming that there is no relationship between smoking and disease would probably be biased if written by a lobbyist for a tobacco company.

3. Is the source up-to-date? For some topics, such as ones associated with current science or technology, up-to-date sources are essential, so check the date on the copyright page of your source. For other topics, the copyright date may be less important or not important at all. If, for example, you were writing about 19th-century pioneer women in Wyoming, the old diaries and letters of such women would be excellent sources.

4. Is the work written at an appropriate level? Materials that are written for children are usually simplified and may be misleading in some respects. Other materials are so technical that they can be understood only after years of study.

5. Does the source come highly recommended? One way to evaluate a source is to ask an expert or authority whether the source is reliable. You can also check the bibliography in a reputable source. If a source is listed in a bibliography, then it is probably considered reliable by the author or editor who put that bibliography together.

Preparing Bibliography Cards

Every time you find a source that might be useful for your research paper, you need to prepare a **bibliography card** for it. All of your bibliography cards, taken together, make up your working bibliography.

A bibliography card serves three basic purposes. First, it enables you to find the source again. Second, it enables you to prepare documentation for your paper. **Documentation** is material included in a research paper to identify the sources from which information was taken. Third, it enables you to prepare the Works Cited list that will appear at the end of your paper.

Journals and other periodicals are particularly good sources for research in science and mathematics because practicing scientists and mathematicians publish their latest findings in such places.

The **Works Cited list** is a complete record of the sources referred to in the paper. Here is a sample bibliography card.

Bibliography card for a book by a single author

Hayashi, Tetsumaro. <u>Steinbeck's Literary Dimension: A Guide to Comparative Studies</u>. Metuchen: Scarecrow, 1973.

① 1

Lucius Beebe Memorial Library   813.08

Notice that a bibliography card contains all or most of the items described below.

1. A bibliographic entry gives essential information about a source, such as its author, its title, the place and/or date of its publication, and the pages (of a book or magazine) on which it was found. The first line of the bibliographic entry begins in the upper left-hand corner of the card. Subsequent lines are indented a few spaces.

2. A source note tells where you found the source. The source listed on the card above was found at the Lucius Beebe Memorial Library. The source note will help you find the source again if you need to do so.

3. A source number is written in the upper right-hand corner of the card and circled. Assign a different number to each source you find. You will use this number to refer to the source on note cards containing material from that source.

4. A card catalog number, if appropriate, should be included. Books and some other materials in libraries are assigned catalog numbers. If your source comes from a library and has a catalog number, you should write that number in the

Research Tip

Arts and Humanities

When doing a paper on an artist or a work of art, don't forget that works of art are themselves your primary sources. Before reading what critics have to say, spend a lot of time with the work of art and take notes on your own reactions to it.

33

lower right-hand corner of the card. The catalog number will help you to find the source again if you need to do so.

Every time you find a possible source, follow these steps.

Research Tip

Language and Literature

When doing a paper on a literary work, consider referring to historical works that deal with the period in which the work was written or to works having to do with the author's life (biographies, journals, collections of letters, etc).

Evaluating and Recording Sources

1. Evaluate the source.

2. Make a bibliography card for it, using a 3" × 5" index card or slip of paper.

3. Find the appropriate bibliography form in Appendix C on pages 82–91. Then write on the card a complete bibliographic entry for the source. Make sure you capitalize and punctuate the entry properly.

4. In the top right-hand corner of the card, record a source number and circle it.

5. At the bottom of the card, record the place where you found the source.

6. If the source has a catalog number, record that number as well.

7. Stack the card with the rest of the cards that make up your working bibliography.

Gathering Information

After you have written a statement of controlling purpose and have prepared a working bibliography, you are ready to begin gathering information for your paper. Begin with the most promising sources recorded in your working bibliography—the ones that are the most general, the most authoritative, or the most accessible. Keeping your controlling purpose clearly in mind, start searching through your sources, looking for relevant information. Do not read, view, or listen to every part of every source. Concentrate on the parts that are relevant to your topic and your purpose.

Some nonprint sources, such as online encyclopedias, have indexes or special search features that can help you to find just the items of information that you need. If you conduct interviews as part of your research, you will be able to prepare questions beforehand to ensure that much of the information that you receive will be related to your topic and purpose.

Preparing Note Cards

There are three basic types of notes:

- A **direct quotation** repeats the words of a source exactly. Quotation marks are used around the quoted material.

- A **paraphrase** states an idea expressed in a source, but not in the same words.

- A **summary** condenses an idea expressed in a source. In other words, it says the same thing in fewer and different words.

Take notes on 4" × 6" cards. Use cards of that size to distinguish your note cards from your 3" × 5" working bibliography cards. Use a separate card for each note so that you can rearrange your notes later on. As a rule of thumb, try to limit each note to one or two sentences on a single idea. Focusing on one idea on

> **"** Do not read, view, or listen to every part of every source. Concentrate on the parts that are relevant to your topic and your purpose. **"**

each card makes it easier to group and reorganize your cards later on.

When you quote, it is extremely important that you copy each letter and punctuation mark exactly. In paraphrasing or summarizing, you need to make sure that when you put the material into your own words, you do not change the source's meaning.

Give a page reference for any information taken from a source, except a dictionary entry or an article in an encyclopedia.

- Information from a single page—write the page number after the note.

- Information from two or more consecutive pages—write the numbers of the first and last pages as follows: 1–4. For consecutive numbers greater than 99, use only the last two digits of the second number, as follows: 110–15.

- Information from nonconsecutive pages in a periodical— write the number of the first page followed by a plus sign, as follows: 76+.

The following note card is well prepared. The note is brief and deals with a single idea. The four main parts of the note card have been labeled.

Source number (Take this number from the appropriate bibliography card.)

Guideline (Keep cards with similar guidelines together.)

Note (This should be a quotation, a paraphrase, a summary, or a combination of those types of notes.)

Page reference (See instructions above.)

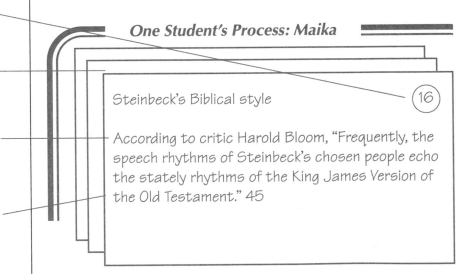

One Student's Process: Maika

Steinbeck's Biblical style   (16)

According to critic Harold Bloom, "Frequently, the speech rhythms of Steinbeck's chosen people echo the stately rhythms of the King James Version of the Old Testament." 45

The following note card needs improvement. It presents two unrelated ideas.

Ancestry of California farm laborers/causes (27)
of the Dust Bowl

"Throughout most of the history of California, its
farm laborers were not European in ancestry. [. . .]
Drought on the Great Plains created a vast dust
bowl where topsoil had literally blown away." 204

This note comes from one page of one source, but it contains two ideas that are only distantly related to one another. The writer needs to use a separate note card for each idea.

The material on this card should be recorded on two separate cards.

Often you may wish to add an explanatory note to a direct quotation in order to identify who said it or to provide necessary background information. Such an explanatory note can be a summary or a paraphrase. The following note, for example, contains a summary that provides a context for the quoted material.

The Joads' idealistic expectations   3

The Joads head to California with high hopes, but
once there they discover that for them "California
is not a Promised Land but a man-blighted Eden."
195

This note begins with a summary that introduces a quotation. Many of your notes will combine quotations with summaries or paraphrases.

The chart on the next page explains when to use the various types of notes.

When doing a research paper on a literary work, it's a good idea to keep a reading journal in which you note important events, supporting quotations, and so on. After reading the work, turn to such secondary sources as books of criticism, author biographies, and articles in scholarly journals.

When to Quote, Paraphrase, or Summarize

1. **Direct quotation.** Use a direct quotation when an idea is especially well stated in a source—that is, when a passage is memorable because of its succinctness, its clarity, its liveliness, its elegance of expression, or another exceptional quality. Also use a direct quotation when the exact wording is important historically, legally, or as a matter of definition.

2. **Paraphrase.** Use the paraphrase as your basic note form—the form that you always use unless you have a good reason to quote or summarize your source.

3. **Summary.** Use summary when a passage in a source is too long to be effectively quoted or paraphrased.

4. **Quotation plus summary or paraphrase.** Write this kind of note when the exact words of the source are desirable but require some explanation in order to be made clear, to be properly attributed, or to be identified as fact or opinion.

The following guidelines will help you to improve your note-taking skills.

Effective Note Taking

1. Keep your topic, controlling purpose, and audience in mind at all times. Do not record material unrelated to your topic.

2. Make sure that summaries and paraphrases accurately express the ideas in your sources.

Effective Note Taking (cont.)

3. Be accurate. Make sure that direct quotations are copied word for word, with capitalization, spelling, and punctuation precisely as in the original. Make sure that every direct quotation begins and ends with quotation marks.

4. Double-check statistics and facts to make sure that you have them right.

5. Distinguish between fact and opinion by labeling opinions as such: "Dr. Graves thinks that . . ." or "According to Grace Jackson . . ."

6. Nonessential parts of a quotation can be cut if the overall meaning of the quotation is not changed. Indicate an omission of material from a quotation by using **ellipsis points**—a series of three spaced dots (. . .)—enclosed in brackets. Use only the three dots when cutting material within a sentence. Use a period before the dots when cutting a full sentence, a paragraph, or more than a paragraph. Use a period after the dots when cutting material from the end of a sentence.

7. Always double-check page references. It's easy to copy these incorrectly.

Avoiding Plagiarism

One of the purposes of your working bibliography and note cards is to help you to avoid plagiarism. **Plagiarism** is the act of intentionally or unintentionally presenting work done by someone else as though it were your own. In most schools, including middle schools, high schools, and universities, plagiarism is considered a serious offense and can result in severe penalties, such as failing grades, loss of course credit, or even expulsion.

Because plagiarism is so serious, it is important to know exactly what it is and what you can do to avoid it. Here is a simple test to determine whether something is plagiarized: ask yourself, Is this information, idea, or statement common knowledge? If the answer is no, then ask yourself, Did this information, idea, or statement come from a source outside myself, or did it come from my own experience or as a result of my own creative activity? If the information, idea, or statement is not common knowledge, and if it came from an outside source, then you must credit that source. Failure to do so constitutes plagiarism.

Developing a Preliminary Outline

At some point early in your research, you will come to know enough about your topic to begin to develop a **preliminary,** or rough, **outline.** A preliminary outline is useful because it will help you to focus your search for information. Your preliminary outline should list some key ideas or subtopics that you expect to include in the body of your paper. As you learn more about your topic, your preliminary outline will change and grow, but even a short, incomplete preliminary outline can be useful.

One Student's Process: Maika

Soon after Maika began her research on *The Grapes of Wrath,* she decided that she might organize her paper by writing first about what happened in real life and then about what happened in the novel. In other words, she would start with the history and then tell Steinbeck's version of it. Rather than writing a complete outline, she started with these two main ideas:

> What happened (the history)
> —the Dust Bowl
> —the migration to California
> Steinbeck's version of it (the novel)
> —the Dust Bowl
> —the migration to California

A preliminary outline can consist of just a few entries or of many. In a preliminary outline, main entries are usually begun at the left-hand margin, and subentries are introduced by dashes.

The Note-Taking/Outlining Cycle

Writing is a cyclical process. At any point in the process, you can stop what you are doing and return to an earlier point. For example, you might decide after doing a bit of research to return to the very beginning and to choose a new topic, or you might decide to change your statement of controlling purpose. In other words, you are free to return to the beginning and to start the writing cycle all over again.

Nowhere in the process of preparing a research paper is the cyclical nature of writing more apparent than in the stage of gathering information. During this stage, you will continually go back and forth between your preliminary outline and your note cards. As you do research and take notes, you will acquire more and more information that you can use to improve your outline. As you change the entries in your outline, you will want to reorganize your note cards, to change the guidelines on the note cards, and to take new notes related to your outline's entries. Your notes and your outline will grow and change together—each feeding into the other.

> **"**Your notes and your outline will grow and change together—each feeding into the other.**"**

Organizing Your Material

I n the preceding chapter you learned that research is a cyclical process. The more research you do, and the more information you gather on note cards, the more you will understand your topic. The more you understand your topic, the more detailed you can make your preliminary outline. The more detailed your preliminary outline becomes, the more you will understand what additional information you need to gather.

At first your preliminary outline will probably be sketchy. However, over time it will become quite detailed. To develop a detailed outline, you will need to consider, over and over again, how best to organize the information that you are gathering. Of course, as you write and research, the organization can and probably will change.

Organizing Ideas in a Research Paper

Much of the writing that people do is fiction, how-to writing, or personal correspondence, and almost all of this writing is organized chronologically. Other writing, including a great deal of nonfiction, is usually organized in what might be called **part-by-part order.** One idea or group of ideas suggests another, which suggests another, and so on to the end. Each idea is related in some way to the one that precedes it and to the one that follows it, but no single, overall method of organization is used.

There are even more possible ways to organize research papers than there are possible topics for such papers. Consequently, there are no hard-and-fast rules about how ideas in research papers should be organized. However, here are some guidelines to keep in mind:

1. Your paper will begin with an introduction that states your thesis. It will end with a conclusion that restates your thesis

> **"** Writing . . . is usually organized in what might be called part-by-part order. One idea or group of ideas suggests another, which suggests another, and so on to the end. **"**

and summarizes the main point or points of the paper. You need to concentrate on organizing the body of the paper. Your goal is to find a sensible method of arranging the information that you will present in the body.

2. Many topics require that you start by providing background information. If you have chosen such a topic, think about what essential background information should appear early on, and group that information together. Among this background information, you might want to include definitions of any key terms that will appear in your paper.

3. Remember that events are usually presented in chronological order unless there is a good reason to present them in some other way. So if part or all of your paper involves presenting events, consider organizing those events chronologically.

4. As you gather your notes, or evidence, sort the note cards into separate piles of related ideas and information. Try different combinations, and make rough outlines based on them.

5. Once you have your note cards separated into piles of related ideas and information, come up with a phrase to describe what is in each pile. Think about the different orders in which you could present each group of ideas. Ask yourself, Should the ideas in pile one be presented first, or those in pile three? Why?

6. Look for relationships among the ideas in each group of note cards. Also look for relationships among groups of cards. The following chart describes some of the relationships that you might discover and build on.

Research Tip

History, Social Studies, Science, and Mathematics

Research papers on topics in these fields often have as their major purpose explaining why something is so or why something occurred or occurs. Therefore, writers of such papers often use cause-and-effect order, at least in part.

Ways to Relate Ideas

1. **Chronological order:** from first event to last event or from last event to first event

2. **Spatial order:** by arrangement in space

3. **Classification:** in groups sharing similar properties or characteristics

A research paper on art may deal with a particular style of art, such as baroque or expressionist or postmodern. A common method of organization is to begin with a definition of the style and then to give examples of it.

Ways to Relate Ideas (cont.)

4. **Order of degree:** according to interest, importance, value, obviousness, certainty, or a similar quality

5. **Cause-and-effect order:** from cause to effect or from effect to cause

6. **Comparison-and-contrast order:** from similarities to differences or from differences to similarities

7. **Analytical order:** according to parts and relationships among the parts

8. **Inductive order, or synthesis:** from specific examples to generalization based on those examples

9. **Deductive order:** from a general idea or principle to specific conclusions based on that general idea or principle

10. **Order of impression, or association:** according to the sequence in which things strike one's attention

11. **Hierarchical order:** from class to subclass (group within a class) or from subclass to class

Creating a Draft Outline

Before beginning your rough draft, you will want to create a draft outline. A **draft outline** is a formal outline that is used as a basis for a rough draft. It can be a **sentence outline,** containing entries that are all complete sentences, or it can be a **topic outline,** containing entries that are words, phrases, or clauses.

A draft outline begins with a statement of controlling purpose. It is divided into two or more major sections introduced by Roman numerals (I, II). Each major section is divided into two or more subsections introduced by capital letters (A, B). The subsections may be divided into sub-subsections introduced by Arabic numerals (1, 2), and those into sub-sub-subsections introduced by lowercase letters (a, b).

One Student's Process: Maika

Maika wrote a draft outline for her paper on Steinbeck's *The Grapes of Wrath*. Maika chose to produce a topic outline.

Topic Outline

<pre>
     The Political Message of John Steinbeck's
                The Grapes of Wrath
Controlling Purpose: The purpose of this
paper is to show that Steinbeck's novel
expressed a strong political message; it
warned that exploitation of migrant workers
would cause them to rise up as a group
against their oppressors, the state and the
wealthy landowners.
   I.   The historical background of the
        migrant situation
        A. The Dust Bowl of the 1930s
        B. The migration to California
        C. The nature of California
           agriculture
        D. The living conditions among the
           migrants
  II.   Steinbeck's opinions about the migrant
        situation
        A. Steinbeck's publication of Their
           Blood Is Strong
        B. Steinbeck's descriptions of the
           migrants' lives
        C. Steinbeck's warning about the
           consequences of exploitation
 III.   Steinbeck's message about the migrant
        situation in The Grapes of Wrath
</pre>

When preparing a formal outline for submission to a teacher or to a peer reviewer, always double-space the outline. On the first page of the outline, include your name, your teacher's name, the name of the class, and the date, as shown in the sample research paper on page 5 of this book. If there are additional pages, include your last name and the page number in the upper right-hand corner of each.

45

A. The Joads as self-absorbed,
   passive victims
B. The Joads as active agents of
   change
C. The conclusion of the novel as a
   warning
D. The title of the novel as a
   parallel between the migrant
   system and Babylon

Here is how the last section would look as a sentence outline:

III. What was Steinbeck's message about the
     migrant situation in <u>The Grapes of
     Wrath</u>?
   A. The Joads began their time of
      struggle as self-absorbed,
      passive victims.
   B. During the struggle, the Joads
      became active agents of change.
   C. The conclusion of the novel is a
      warning.
   D. The title of the novel draws a
      parallel between the migrant
      system and Babylon.

Drafting Your Research Paper

After completing a draft outline and arranging your note cards to match the outline, you are ready to begin writing your rough draft. The comforting thing about a rough draft is that it does not have to be perfect. You can rework your draft as often as you like and watch it take shape gradually. In other words, you do not have to hit a home run your first time at bat. You can have as many chances at the plate as you want.

Approaches to Drafting

With regard to drafting, writers fall into two major camps. Some prefer to get everything down on paper quickly, but in very rough form, and then do one or more detailed revisions. Others like to complete each section as they go, writing and polishing one section, then moving on to the next. Either approach is acceptable. If you choose the second approach, however, you might want to look first at pages 57–62, which deal with revision.

The Style of the Draft

A research paper is a type of objective, formal writing. Therefore, you should avoid making the paper personal and subjective, and you should avoid using informal language. Do not use such words as *I, me, my, mine, we,* and *our.* Do not state opinions without supporting them with facts. Do not use slang, colloquialisms, nonstandard dialect, or contractions.

Assembling the Draft

A rough draft is just that—it is rough, or unfinished. As you draft, do not worry about matters that you can take care of later, such as details of spelling, grammar, usage, and mechanics.

> **"**You do not have to hit a home run your first time at bat. You can have as many chances at the plate as you want.**"**

Instead, concentrate on getting your ideas down in an order that makes sense.

Use your outline as a guide. Explore each main point, supporting the idea with evidence from your note cards. When you use information from a note card in your draft, write the source number from the note card and circle it. Noting the source number is extremely important because during revision you will have to find the source in order to document it.

One Student's Process: Maika

One of the entries in Maika's outline for her paper on John Steinbeck was the following:

```
The migration to California
```

Maika turned this entry into a statement, which she used as a topic sentence:

```
The Dust Bowl led to a massive
migration, or movement, of people from
Oklahoma to California.
```

Then she added material from her note cards to support the topic sentence:

```
The Dust Bowl led to a massive
migration. People went from Oklahoma to
California--300,000 to 400,000 homeless
farmers from the Dust Bowl area packed
everything into old cars or trucks and
headed to California to find work (13) . The
panhandle region lost more than half its
residents. But when they got to
California, they did not find paradise.
They found "not a Promised Land but a
man-blighted Eden" (3) .
```

Notice that Maika added both paraphrased and quoted material. In each case she included a source number from a note card so that she would be able to find information about the source later on, when she was preparing the documentation, or full source information, for her paper.

Incorporating summaries and paraphrases. Working summaries and paraphrases into your paper is quite easy. Simply write them out as part of your text and include a source number at the end of the summarized or paraphrased material. Just be certain to use transitions to connect the material smoothly to the sentences that precede or follow it.

Incorporating quotations. Working quotations into your paper is a bit more complicated because there are many ways in which quotations can be used. Also, the rules for prose differ from those for poetry or song lyrics. See the chart on pages 50–51 for complete instructions on using quotations in your draft.

The Draft as a Work in Progress

As you write, you may occasionally discover gaps in the information that you have gathered. In other words, you may find that you do not have in your note cards all the information you need to make some point. When this occurs, you can stop and look for the information, or you can simply make a note to yourself to find the information later on. Either approach is acceptable.

The need to fill gaps is one example of a general characteristic of drafting: that drafting is still discovery time. In addition to discovering gaps to be filled, you may discover better ways to organize parts of the paper, contradictions in your source materials, or significant parts of your topic that you have not yet explored. You may even find a whole new approach to your topic, one more interesting or workable than the one you have taken. Remain open to the discoveries that occur as you draft. Be willing to return, if necessary, to earlier stages of the writing process to do more research, to revise your controlling purpose, or to change your outline.

> **"**Drafting is still discovery time.**"**

49

Quoting Prose Works

1. If the quotation is four lines long or less, put it in quotation marks and place it in the text of your paper:

    An actress who visited one of the migrant camps wrote, "I went around in a sick daze for hours after witnessing unimaginable suffering" (13).

    The circled number is the source number from your note card. When you do your final documentation, you will replace this number with a citation in parentheses. (See pages 63–70.)

2. You do not have to quote complete sentences:

    An actress who visited one of the migrant camps wrote of seeing "unimaginable suffering" (13).

3. You can also break a quotation into two parts:

    "I went around in a sick daze for hours," wrote an actress who visited a camp, "after witnessing unimaginable suffering" (13).

4. When a quoted passage is more than four lines long, set it off from the text of your paper. Put a colon after the statement that introduces the quotation. Begin a new line. Indent the entire quotation ten spaces from the left-hand margin. Double-space the quotation, and do not enclose it in quotation marks:

    The extent of the desperation is made clear in a report written in 1939, the year that The Grapes of Wrath was published:

    > The State Relief Administration estimates that most agricultural workers only have employment for six months in the year or less; and that the average yearly earnings per family [. . . were] $289 in 1935. (17)

5. When quoting more than one paragraph, indent the first line of each full paragraph an additional three spaces. However, indent the first sentence only if it begins a paragraph in your source.

Quoting Prose Works (cont.)

```
The migrants also faced an even more terrible problem:
        There has been no war in California, no
        plague, no bombing of open towns and roads,
        no shelling of cities. It is a beautiful
        year. And thousands of families are
        starving. [. . .]
        [It's] in the tents you see along the
        roads and in the shacks built from dump heap
        materials that the hunger is, and it isn't
        malnutrition. It is starvation. (19)
```

Quoting Poetry, Verse Plays, and Songs

1. When quoting a single line or part of a line, simply place the material in your text with quotation marks around it:

```
Shakespeare's Macbeth says, "Life's but a walking
shadow" (4).
```

2. When quoting two or three lines, separate the lines with a space, a slash (/), and another space:

```
Shakespeare's Macbeth says: "Life's but a walking
shadow, a poor player, / That struts and frets his hour
upon the stage / And then is heard no more" (4).
```

3. When quoting four or more lines, set the material off from your text. Indent it ten spaces, double-space it, and do not enclose it in quotation marks. Follow the line division and spacing of the original.

```
Shakespeare's Macbeth says:
        Life's but a walking shadow, a poor player,
        That struts and frets his hour upon the stage
        And then is heard no more. It is a tale
        Told by an idiot, full of sound and fury,
        Signifying nothing. (4)
```

Using Graphic Aids

As you draft, stay alert to the possibility of using tables, maps, charts, diagrams, and other **graphic aids** to present information concisely. If you use a graphic aid from a source, or if you use information from a source to create a graphic aid, then you must credit the source of the information.

Tables should be labeled "Table 1," "Table 2," and so on. Other graphic aids should be labeled "Fig. 1," "Fig. 2," and so on. Place the label after the figure and follow it with a caption that is either the title or a description of the graphic aid. Follow that with a source credit in endnote form (see pages 94–101).

One Student's Process: Marcus

Marcus was doing a paper on the attack of the African-American Massachusetts 54th Infantry Regiment on the Confederate stronghold of Fort Wagner, South Carolina, during the Civil War. His completed paper is on pages 105–111. Here is a graphic that Marcus created on the basis of a map that he found while doing his research.

Fig. 1. Charleston
harbor, 1863.
Adapted from
Peter Burchard,
<u>One Gallant
Rush: Robert
Gould Shaw and
His Brave Black
Regiment</u> (New
York: St.
Martin's, 1965)
110.

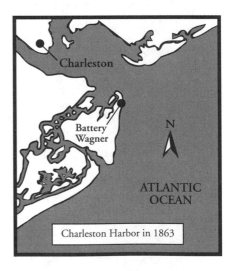

52

The introduction of a research paper should accomplish two purposes:

1. It should grab the reader's attention.

2. It should present the paper's main idea, or **thesis statement.**

In addition, the introduction may define key terms, supply necessary background information, or both. The introduction can be of any length, although most introductions are one or two paragraphs long.

Capturing the Reader's Attention

There are many ways to capture a reader's attention in an introduction. You can begin with a startling or unusual fact, with a question, with an anecdote (a brief story that makes a point), with an analogy (a comparison between the topic and something with which the reader is already familiar), with a paragraph that compares or contrasts, or with examples.

Writing the Thesis Statement

To create your thesis statement, you can simply recast your statement of controlling purpose. You may decide to change the statement, however, to reflect any additional refining or refocusing of your topic that has occurred during research. However, avoid using the phrase "the purpose of this paper" in your final thesis statement. Notice how that phrase is eliminated in the following example:

> Controlling Purpose: The purpose of this paper is to show that Steinbeck's novel expressed a strong political message; it warned that exploitation of migrant workers would cause them to rise up as a group against their oppressors, the state and the wealthy landowners.

> " The introduction of a research paper should . . . grab the reader's attention [and] . . . present the paper's main idea, or thesis statement. "

```
Thesis Statement: Steinbeck's The Grapes
of Wrath warned that exploitation of
migrant workers would cause them to rise
up as a group against their oppressors,
the state and the wealthy landowners. But
beyond that, the novel shows how such an
oppressive situation can result in a
profound philosophical change in the
people who experience it.
```

Sometimes, in order for your reader to understand your thesis statement, you will have to provide some additional background information. In the introduction all you need to include is enough information to help the reader understand the thesis. You can provide additional information in the body of your paper.

One Student's Process: Marcus

Marcus's thesis statement for his paper on the Massachusetts 54th Infantry Regiment was, "Although many Yankee soldiers lost their lives in the charge on Fort Wagner, and although the Confederates technically won the battle, the charge of the Massachusetts 54th was a great victory for the North and for the antislavery movement." Since a reader might never have heard of the Massachusetts 54th or of Fort Wagner, Marcus decided to open with some background information:

```
     On July 18, 1863, at the height of the
Civil War, the African-American men of the
54th Massachusetts Infantry Regiment attacked
a South Carolina earthwork known as Fort
Wagner or Battery Wagner. When the fighting
was done, nearly half of those men lay dead
in what was by all accounts a massacre, an
```

overwhelming victory for the Confederacy ⑧ .
However, the African-American soldiers of
the 54th had fought as free men. So although
many of these Yankee soldiers lost their
lives in the charge, and although the
Confederates technically won the battle, the
charge of the Massachusetts 54th was a
moral, if not a military, victory for the
North and for the antislavery movement.

One Student's Process: Maika

In her introduction, Maika wanted to accomplish two
purposes: she wanted to introduce the concept of the
political novel, and she wanted to state her thesis, or
main idea. She decided to begin with a comparison and
some examples to clarify what a political novel is:

A novel, like a movie, is a form of
entertainment. However, some novels do a
great deal more than entertain. Some pack a
powerful political message. For example,
Uncle Tom's Cabin, by Harriet Beecher Stowe,
created controversy from the moment it was
published. The Jungle, by Upton Sinclair,
alerted the country to the horrors of the
meatpacking industry.

Then, in the last two sentences of her second paragraph,
Maika introduced her thesis statement:

John Steinbeck's The Grapes of Wrath is
another example of a novel with a powerful
political message. It warned that
exploitation of migrant workers would cause

55

them to rise up as a group against their
oppressors, the state and the wealthy
landowners. Beyond that, the novel showed
how such an oppressive situation can result
in a profound philosophical change in the
people who experience it. Steinbeck
demonstrated this by showing how one migrant
family becomes politicized.

Writing the Conclusion

Like an introduction, a conclusion is usually one or two paragraphs long. The most common way to conclude a research paper is to restate the main idea and the principal arguments presented to support that idea. In addition, you may wish to use the conclusion to tie up any loose ends left in the body of your paper, to explain the consequences of accepting the thesis statement, to call on the reader to take some action, to explain the importance or value of what the reader has learned from the paper, or to make predictions about the future. The conclusion is an opportunity to be imaginative. Almost anything is acceptable as long as it leaves the reader satisfied that the treatment of the subject has been complete. (See the sample conclusions on pages 17 and 109 of this book.)

> **"The conclusion is an opportunity to be imaginative. Almost anything is acceptable as long as it leaves the reader satisfied that the treatment of the subject has been complete."**

Revising Your Research Paper

After you finish drafting your research paper, put it aside for a day or so. Distancing yourself from the paper will help you to view it more objectively in preparation for revising it.

Expect the revision of your paper to take several days, and expect to revise your paper more than once. One excellent approach is to do separate revisions for content and organization, for style, and for documentation. During revision, do not worry about details of spelling, grammar, usage, and mechanics. You can clean up problems in those areas later on, during the proofreading stage. With regard to documentation, all you have to worry about at this point is having a source number in your manuscript for every instance where you have used a source. The next chapter will explain how to turn the source numbers into complete, final documentation.

Peer Response

At some point during the drafting process, give your paper to one of your peers, or fellow students, for review. By having a peer review your paper, you can find out whether you've fulfilled your purpose, whether you have been completely clear, and whether there are parts that cause problems for readers.

Do not worry about losing control of your work. You have the right to accept or reject any suggestions that your peer reviewer makes. Here are some questions you can ask your peer reviewer to elicit useful responses from him or her.

Questions for Peer Readers

- What do you think my main point, or thesis, is? Do you think I have proved that point? Why or why not? What could I do to make the proof more complete?

- Which sections of the paper did you find most interesting or informative?

- Were any parts of the paper unclear to you?

- What questions do you have about my topic now that you have read my paper?

Self-Evaluation

A peer reviewer's comments can give you important insights into how your paper can be improved. However, it is also important that you perform your own close evaluation of the paper. Ask yourself the questions in the following checklist.

Revision Checklist

CONTENT AND ORGANIZATION

General

☐ **1.** Does my paper adequately support or prove my thesis statement?

☐ **2.** Does my paper have a clear introduction, body, and conclusion?

☐ **3.** Does every idea follow logically from the one that precedes it?

☐ **4.** Have I used transitions to show connections between ideas?

Introduction

☐ **5.** Will the introduction capture my reader's attention?

☐ **6.** Does the introduction present my thesis statement clearly?

Body

☐ **7.** Does the body of my paper present evidence from a variety of reliable sources?

☐ **8.** Is information from my sources presented in a combination of summary, paraphrase, and quotation?

☐ **9.** Are there any gaps in my argument that I need to fill by doing additional research? Are there any points that are inadequately supported?

☐ **10.** Have I deleted all unnecessary or irrelevant material from my paper?

☐ **11.** Have I avoided unsubstantiated statements of opinion throughout?

Conclusion

☐ **12.** Did I restate my thesis in the conclusion of my paper?

☐ **13.** Does the conclusion summarize the main points that I have presented in support of the thesis?

☐ **14.** Does the conclusion give my reader a sense of completion? (Are all the loose ends tied up? Have all the parts of the thesis been supported? Have all of a reader's most likely questions about the topic been addressed?)

STYLE

☐ **15.** Have I varied my writing by using many kinds of sentences—short and long sentences; simple, compound, complex, and compound-complex sentences; declarative, exclamatory, and interrogative sentences; and sentences that begin with different parts of speech?

☐ **16.** Have I avoided wordiness? Have I deleted unnecessary words, phrases, and clauses?

☐ **17.** Have I used clear, concrete examples? Have I defined key terms?

18. Have I avoided informal language, slang, and technical words that I have not defined? Have I avoided contractions, personal references, and first-person pronouns such as *I, we, me,* and *our?*

19. Are the sentences in the paper graceful, not awkward?

DOCUMENTATION

20. Have I avoided plagiarism by completely documenting all material taken from sources? Does every summary, paraphrase, or quotation have a corresponding source number?

21. Is each of my direct quotations set off with quotation marks or by indention? Is each quotation accurate? Does it reflect precisely the meaning that the author of the source intended?

22. Is there a complete bibliography card, in proper form, for every source number in the final version of my manuscript? (For information on proper bibliographic form, see pages 82–91.)

One Student's Process: Maika

Maika wrote a rough draft of her paper on John Steinbeck's *The Grapes of Wrath*. Then she revised the draft for content and organization. In one paragraph, she added additional information to support her topic sentence and to clarify the meaning of the term *Dust Bowl.* She replaced the pronoun *he* with a proper noun to make clear whom she was writing about. She moved a sentence to improve the paragraph's organization, and she cut a sentence that was irrelevant to her topic.

The Grapes of Wrath is a historical novel ∧ ^a summation of national experience at a given time. Therefore,

we should recognize that it is important to □

understand the historical events on which the

novel was based, ~~before one can understand the~~

~~novel.~~ The historical and economic experience □

that ~~he~~ Steinbeck was reacting to was ∧ that of the migrents who left

the Oklahoma Dust Bowl in the late 1930s (12) . ∧ Storms blew away topsoil (27) covered pastures and suffocated livestock (23)

Crop failure, added to already low crop prices, led to the foreclosure of many small

farms and the homelessness of many farm families"

(27) . At that time the country was in the middle of

a bad period called the great depression. ~~Many~~ □ which had reduced the prices farmers could charge for crops.

~~businesses in the East also closed during the~~

~~Depression.~~

One Student's Process: Maika

Then Maika revised her paragraph for style. She deleted unnecessary words, removed a first-person pronoun, reordered a sentence to make it less awkward, and replaced the vague term *bad period* with a concrete, specific phrase.

Finally, Maika fixed the remaining problems in her documentation. She added a missing source number and some missing quotation marks, and she fixed a sentence that she had quoted inaccurately, adding a word that she had accidentally dropped. When she proofread the final version of her paper, Maika corrected the remaining errors in spelling, grammar, and mechanics. Compare the revised paragraph on the preceding page with Maika's final version on pages 5–6 of this book.

Preparing a Final Outline

Your teacher may ask you to submit a final outline along with the final draft of your paper. If so, revise the last version of your draft outline, being sure to follow the guidelines for outlining given on pages 44–46. In most cases either a topic outline or a sentence outline is acceptable, although your teacher may prefer one type of outline over the other. The final outline should be typed or prepared on a word processor. For information on proper manuscript form for the outline and for the rest of the paper, see pages 74–75 of this book.

Documenting Your Sources

8

Each time you use information from your note cards, write down a source number. After you revise your draft, use the source numbers in the revised draft to prepare your documentation. **Documentation** is the information in the paper that tells what sources you used.

Parenthetical Documentation

The method of documentation most widely used today is called **parenthetical documentation.** This method has largely replaced documentation with endnotes or footnotes. (For information on endnotes, footnotes, and other methods of documentation, see Appendix D on pages 92–112.)

To acknowledge a source with parenthetical documentation, enclose a brief reference in parentheses. The reference, which is called a **parenthetical citation,** usually consists of an author's name and a page number:

```
The Grapes of Wrath is a historical novel, "a

summation of national experience at a given

time" (Levant 93).
```

The process of placing the citation in your paper is called **citing a source.**

A parenthetical citation contains just enough information to help the reader locate the source in the Works Cited list at the end of your paper. The Works Cited list consists of bibliographic entries like those shown in Appendix C on pages 82–91.

Take a moment to look at the sample research paper on pages 5–17. Study the examples of parenthetical citations throughout the paper. Then look at the Works Cited list on pages 18–19, at the end of the sample paper.

Preparing Parenthetical Citations

Preparing parenthetical citations to document your sources is fairly straightforward; and by creating them, you make your sources easily accessible to your reader. The following guidelines will help you to cite your sources properly:

1. Basic citation. Place the citation at the end of the sentence that contains the material you are documenting. The citation should appear after the last word of the sentence but before the end mark.

```
The Oklahoma migrants found "not a Promised
Land but a man-blighted Eden" (Crockett 195).
```

2. Citation of a long quotation. When documenting a long quotation that is set off from the text, place the citation after the end punctuation.

```
    No one is really certain about the origins
of the term "Dust Bowl":
        H. L. Mencken in a footnote to the
        first supplement (1945) to his
        monumental The American Language
        traces the term [. . .] to an
        Associated Press dispatch sent by
        staff writer Robert Geiger from
        Guymon, Oklahoma, on April 15, 1935.
        (French, Companion 3)
```

3. Basic citation with author's name in text. If the name of the author is clear from the context in which the parenthetical reference appears, then give only the page number.

```
    As H. Kelly Crockett has pointed out, the
Oklahoma migrants found "not a Promised Land
but a man-blighted Eden" (195).
```

4. Citation of multiple works by one author.

If the Works Cited list contains more than one work by the author, then include an abbreviated version of the title. When abbreviating a title, drop small opening words like *a, an,* or *the,* begin with the word that the full title would be alphabetized by, and reduce the overall length to one to four words. So, for example, the title *A Companion to* The Grapes of Wrath might become *Companion.*

The success of <u>The Grapes of Wrath</u> overshadowed
Steinbeck's later work (French, <u>Companion</u> ix).

5. Citation with author's name and title in text.

If the name of the author and the title of the work both appear in the text of your paper, use only the page number, even if more than one work by the author is listed in your Works Cited list.

In "The Commonplace and the Grotesque," critic
Edwin Bowdin points out that Steinbeck's novel
contains people who are "isolated and lonely
and even grotesque" (16).

6. Citation of a work available in various editions.

When citing a literary work available in different editions, include information that will allow the reader to find the quotation in any edition. For a novel, include a chapter number.

One character in Steinbeck's novel points out
that "Everybody says words different. [. . .]
Arkansas folks says 'em different, and Oklahomy
folks says 'em different. And we seen a lady
from Massachusetts, an' she said 'em
differentest of all" (173; ch. 13).

For a short story or essay, include a paragraph number: ("Meditation 17" 300; par. 7). For a play divided into acts and scenes, give the act number and the scene number, separated by a period. Omit the page number(s). If the play is printed with line numbering, include line numbers as well: (<u>Macbeth</u> 5.5. 24–28).

7. Citation of an anonymous work. When citing an anonymous work (one for which no author is identified), give an abbreviated version of the title, followed by the page number. Make sure that the first word in the abbreviated title is the word by which the work is alphabetized in the Works Cited list. Here is a citation for an anonymous work called "Some Factual Errors in Steinbeck's Portrayal of Oklahoma and Oklahomans."

```
One contributor wrote that the novel contained

"a number of factual errors" ("Some Factual

Errors" 647).
```

8. Citation of an encyclopedia or a similar reference work. When citing an article in a reference work that is arranged alphabetically—an article in an encyclopedia or in a biographical dictionary, for example—give only the title or a shortened version of the title.

```
One cause of the Dust Bowl was misuse of the

land ("Dust Bowl").
```

9. Citation of a work by two or three authors. When citing a work by two or three authors, give the authors' last names and the page number.

```
Very little is now known about how dolphins and

whales communicate (Akmajian, Demers, and

Harnish 36).
```

10. Citation of a work by more than three authors. When citing a work by more than three authors, give the last name of the first author, followed by *et al.* and the page number. *Et al.* is an abbreviation of Latin *et alii* or *et aliae,* meaning "and others."

```
Scientists are still debating whether the

higher apes can be taught to create "sentences"

in sign language (Kim et al. 427).
```

Research Tip

Science and Mathematics

Scientists often use a variation of the parenthetical-documentation system known as the **author-date system.** For information on that system, see pages 102–103.

11. Citation of a quotation appearing in a source.

When citing a statement that is quoted by your source, use the abbreviation *qtd. in.*

```
An actress who visited one of these camps

wrote, "I went around in a sick daze for hours

after witnessing unimaginable suffering" (qtd.

in Stein 219).
```

12. Citation of a nonpaginated source.

For a source without page numbers—an interview, a piece of computer software, or a recording, for example—give the name of the author or interviewee. If there is no name, give the title or a shortened version of the title.

```
The migrants didn't have the necessary money,

or "Do-Re-Me," to live decently (Guthrie).
```

13. Citation of a multivolume work.

To cite a page number in a multivolume work that is *not* an alphabetically organized reference work, give the author's name, the volume number, a colon, and the page reference.

```
Today, specialists in language often use the

term grammar to refer to any aspect of language

that can be described systematically (Lyons

2:378).
```

14. Citation of more than one page.

When citing more than one page, use a hyphen to separate the numbers unless the pages are nonconsecutive.

```
French points out that "The Grapes of Wrath has

been applauded throughout the world since its

publication" (Companion 147-48).
```

When citing consecutive pages, give the complete form of the second number for numbers through 99: 1–2, 13–15, 35–36, 67–69. When citing larger numbers, give only the last two digits of the second number unless more digits are required for clarity's sake: 99–102, 117–18, 223–24, 1201–02, 1201–303.

Preparing the Works Cited List

Each time you cite a source in your paper, pull the bibliography card for that source from your working bibliography and place it in a new stack of Works Cited cards. When you have completed the final draft of your paper, you will have a complete set of Works Cited cards. Arrange those cards in alphabetical order. Then type up your final Works Cited list from the cards, following their style exactly. Your final Works Cited list should include a complete entry for every source that you have cited in your paper. Here is a sample Works Cited list for a research paper on saving forests.

Pappas 23

Works Cited

Caldicott, Helen. If You Love This Planet:
    A Plan to Heal the Earth. New York:
    Norton, 1992.

Dietrich, William. The Final Forest: The
    Battle for the Last Great Trees of the
    Pacific Northwest. New York: Simon,
    1992.

Frome, Michael. Regreening the National
    Parks. Tucson: U of Arizona P, 1992.

Hamilton, Harriet. "From Stones and Clay
    an Abundance of Trees."
    Conservationist Sep.-Oct. 1991: 32-35.

Harrison, Robert Pogue. Forests: The
    Shadow of Civilization. Chicago: U of
    Chicago P, 1992.

Kahak, E. "Perceiving the Good." <u>The</u>
    <u>Wilderness Condition: Essays on</u>
    <u>Environment and Civilization</u>. Ed. Max
    Oelschaeger. San Francisco: Sierra
    Club, 1992. 173-87.
Kernan, Henry S. "The World Is My Woodlot
    Too." <u>Conservationist</u> Jan.-Feb. 1992:
    44-47.
Ketchledge, Edwin H. "Born-Again Forest."
    <u>Natural History</u> May 1992: 34-38.
Sebesta, Lou. "Balmville Tree." <u>New York</u>
    <u>State Conversationist</u> Apr. 1999. 5
    Oct. 1999 <http://www.dec.state.ny.us/
    website/dpae/cons/balmvilletree.html>.
Snyder, Gary. "Etiquette of Freedom." <u>The</u>
    <u>Wilderness Condition: Essays on</u>
    <u>Environment and Civilization</u>. Ed. Max
    Oelschaeger. San Francisco: Sierra
    Club, 1992. 21-39.

If you use more than one work by the same author, put them in alphabetical order. Give the author's name for the first work. Thereafter, use three hyphens in place of the name.

Steinbeck, John. <u>The Grapes of Wrath</u>.
    1939. New York: Penguin, 1999.
---. <u>Their Blood Is Strong</u>. San Francisco:
    Lubin, 1938. Rpt.in French, <u>Companion</u>
    53-92.

"Your final Works Cited list should include a complete entry for every source that you have cited in your paper."

If you use several pieces from a collection of a single author's works, you can give an entry for the entire work, without listing the individual essays or articles.

Manuscript Form for the Works Cited List

1. Begin on a new page.

2. Use one-inch margins on both sides.

3. Include your last name and the page number, flush right, half an inch from the top of the page.

4. Drop down another one-half inch and center the title "Works Cited." Do not underline it or use all capital letters.

5. Double-space between entries. Double-space between the title and the first entry.

6. Begin each entry at the left margin. Double-space within each entry. Indent run-over lines five spaces from the left margin.

7. If you wish, you can break down your Works Cited list into categories such as "Books," "Periodicals," and so on. If you do this, list the materials under each heading alphabetically.

9

Completing Your Research Paper

After you have finished your documentation, you are ready to proofread your paper and to prepare your final manuscript. **Proofreading** is the process of checking your paper for errors in spelling, grammar, usage, level of language, capitalization, punctuation, and documentation. The **final manuscript** is the copy of your paper that will be read by your teacher and by others.

Proofreading Your Paper

The first step after revising your paper and preparing your documentation is proofreading it to eliminate errors. When you proofread, use symbols like those shown on page 76. The following guidelines are particularly important to keep in mind when proofreading a research paper.

Proofreading a Research Paper

1. Double-check the spellings of proper names, such as the names of people and places.

2. Check to see that the quotations that you have used fit grammatically into the sentences in which they appear.

   Ungrammatical: In the 1930s the migrants truly did "harvesting the grapes of wrath."

   Grammatical: In the 1930s the migrants truly were "harvesting the grapes of wrath."

Proofreading a Research Paper (cont.)

3. Check to see that your language is appropriately formal.

4. Check all titles of works to make sure that these rules have been followed:

   • They appear in uppercase and lowercase letters. (Titles should not be written in all capital letters.)

   • All adjectives, adverbs, gerunds, interjections, nouns, participles, pronouns, subordinating conjunctions, and verbs are capitalized, along with the first and last words and words that follow colons.

   • They are punctuated properly.

5. Check every sentence to make sure that it has an end mark. If the sentence ends with a parenthetical citation, make sure that the citation appears before the end mark, except in the case of a long, indented quotation, where the citation should follow the end mark.

6. Check every quotation in the body of the text to make sure that it begins and ends with quotation marks. Make sure that quotations within quotations in the body of the text are enclosed in single quotation marks. If a quotation is more than four lines long, it should be set off from the body of the text and indented, without quotation marks.

7. Check that you have used ellipsis points properly in edited quotations. (See page 39.)

8. Make sure that every quotation, summary, or paraphrase is followed by a parenthetical citation. Make sure that every citation corresponds to an entry in the Works Cited list.

9. Check every quotation against your note cards to make sure that it is accurate.

Preparing the Final Manuscript

After proofreading, you need to prepare your final manuscript. A recommended manuscript form for research papers is described on the next two pages. You may also wish to refer to the sample research paper on pages 5–19.

After preparing the final manuscript, proofread it one last time. Mark any corrections neatly on the manuscript, using the proofreading symbols shown in the chart on page 76. If a page contains more than three corrections, consider creating a new final page.

Finally, get together all the work that your teacher wishes to see—your paper, including the Works Cited list, and possibly your final outline, your note cards, and your bibliography cards. Congratulations! You have just finished your research paper.

Reflecting on the Process

Do some thinking about your experience of writing your paper while it is still fresh in your mind. If you reflect now, you may think of some ways to save yourself time as you work on your next research paper. In your journal, write about your research experience. Consider such questions as, What have I learned? What parts of the research process were easiest or most difficult for me? What would I do differently next time?

Guidelines for Manuscript Form: Research Papers

1. **General guidelines/type of paper.** If possible, type or word-process your paper. Use high-quality white, unlined 8½" × 11" paper. Do not use colored paper, transparent paper, onionskin paper, or odd type-faces such as script. For information on using word-processing programs for research papers, see Appendix A on pages 77–78.

   If you must write your paper out by hand, print or use cursive writing, whichever is neater. Use lined paper, write on only one side of each sheet, and follow the same format guidelines that you would follow when typing or word processing.

2. **Margins.** Use one-inch margins at the top, sides, and bottom of each page.

3. **Name and page numbers.** Place your last name, a space, and the page number at the top of each page of the paper. The name and page number should appear one-half inch from the top edge of the page, flush with the right-hand margin. Number the pages of the paper and the Works Cited list continuously, using Arabic numerals (1, 2, 3, and so on). Do not precede the page numbers with the word *page* or any abbreviation of it, such as *p.,* or *pg.*

4. **Spacing.** Double-space the entire paper, including headings, titles, quotations, and text paragraphs.

5. **Heading.** At the left margin of the first page, drop down one inch from the top edge of the sheet and enter, on separate lines, your complete name, your teacher's name, the name of your class, and the complete date in this form: 12 November 2000. Double-space between the lines.

6. **Title.** On the line following the date, center the title of your paper. Use uppercase and lowercase letters, not all capitals, and underline only those words, such as the titles of long works, that you would underline in the body of your paper. Double-space between the date and the title and between the title and the first paragraph of the paper.

Guidelines for Manuscript Form:
Research Papers (cont.)

7. **Indentions.** Indent the first line of each text paragraph in your paper five spaces from the left margin.

8. **Quotations.** See the guidelines for quotations on pages 50–51.

9. **Paragraphing.** Do not leave a single line of a paragraph at the bottom or the top of a page.

10. **Works Cited list.** On the first Works Cited page, after your last name and the page number, drop down an additional one-half inch to a position one inch from the top edge of the sheet, and center the title "Works Cited." Do not underline the title or enclose it in quotation marks.

11. **Placement and spacing of Works Cited entries.** Double-space after the title "Works Cited" and begin the first Works Cited entry.

    Double-space and alphabetize all the Works Cited entries. Entries should be alphabetized by their first words, whether the words are parts of titles or of persons' names. If an entry begins with a title, skip any initial article (*a, an,* or *the*) when alphabetizing.

    Begin the first line of each Works Cited entry at the left margin. Indent subsequent lines five spaces.

12. **Binding and presentation.** Do not staple your research paper, and do not use rubber bands. Follow the instructions for binding and presentation given by your teacher. Most teachers will ask that you fasten the pages together with a paper clip.

13. **Final outline.** If your teacher asks you to submit a final outline along with your research paper, use one of the formats shown in the sample outlines on pages 45–46. In your final outline, however, replace your statement of controlling purpose with your thesis statement.

Proofreading Symbols

N̶orth of Mexico	Make lowercase.
President jefferson	Capitalize.
a fine t̶h̶i̶n̶g̶ *idea*	Replace.
this t̶h̶i̶s̶ time	Delete.
thi̶e̶r̶	Transpose.
1, 2ʌ or 3	Add a comma.
Letʼs go.	Add an apostrophe.
Welcome, friends⊙	Add a period.
They ʌ leaving. *are*	Add letters or words.

76

Computers and the Research Paper

If you have access to a personal computer at home or at school, consider using it to prepare your research paper. The following are some suggestions about how a personal computer can be used in the various stages of the research process:

1. **Finding sources.** Many libraries have computerized catalogs that can help you to find sources. You can also use a personal computer to find information directly (see items 2 and 3 below).

2. **Using commercial online services.** Of particular value as sources of information are commercial online information services. These services offer current facts and news; online encyclopedias; access to abstracts or full versions of periodicals, reports, and government documents; homework assistance; tutoring; classes in particular subjects; and research assistance. A few of the online services offer connections to libraries and museums, including the Library of Congress and the Smithsonian Institution in Washington, D.C. To use an online service, you need either a computer with a modem linked to a telephone line or a television set with an Internet-ready box. Your school's computer lab or resource center may be linked to a commercial online service.

3. **Using computer networks.** Some local school districts and some states have special education networks that connect students, teachers, and administrators. An example of such a network is the TENET, or Texas Education Network, which is itself connected to the Internet, a massive computer network that connects businesses, universities, and government research centers around the globe. A computer that is linked to the Internet gives you access to a huge number of information sources. For example, sites on the World Wide Web—one of the most popular Internet resources—can be good sources of up-to-the-minute information. Your school's computer lab may be linked to the Internet or to other state or local networks.

4. **Using CD-ROMs.** If you have access to a CD-ROM drive, you will be able to use some of the many resource materials—from timetables of history or science to encyclopedias to the works of Shakespeare—that are available on CD-ROM. See your local computer dealer about purchasing such discs, or see if your school or community library has a CD-ROM collection.

5. **Preparing computerized bibliography cards and note cards.** You can use database or hypertext programs to prepare note cards and bibliography cards. The advantage of preparing note cards and bibliography cards with such programs is that you can sort the cards automatically, in alphabetical or numerical order, according to any element in them, such as the names of authors or editors, the guidelines, or the source numbers.

6. **Using documentation software.** Several programs are now available that generate bibliographies, Works Cited lists , endnotes, and footnotes automatically, and some word-processing programs have built-in documentation features. However, before you use such a program, make sure that it follows the style that is specified in this book—the style described in the *MLA Handbook for Writers of Research Papers.*

7. **Using outlining software.** Many word-processing programs have built-in outlining features. Separate outlining programs are also available. However, be careful that any program that you use creates outlines in the form described in this book or in a form acceptable to your teacher.

8. **Creating graphics.** Personal computers can, of course, be used to prepare graphics for use in research papers. Excellent programs exist for drawing, for creating charts and tables, for creating graphs of all kinds, and for mapping.

Abbreviations for Use in Research Papers

Dates and Geographic Names

See a dictionary or the *MLA Handbook for Writers of Research Papers* for abbreviations of days, months, and geographic names.

Publishers

When including publishers' names in Works Cited entries, footnotes, or endnotes, leave out articles (*a, an, the*), abbreviations of business entities (*Co., Inc., Ltd.*), and words that describe the business that the publishers are in (*Books, House, Press, Publishers*). However, use the abbreviations *U* for "University" and *P* for "Press" in Works Cited entries for university-press publications, as in *MIT P, U of Texas P, U of Puerto Rico P,* and *Cambridge UP.*

Use the following accepted shortened forms of publishers' names. If a publishing-house name consists of a person's name (Jeremy P. Tarcher, Inc.), then use the last name as the shortened form (Tarcher). If the publisher does not appear in the following list or if the name of the publishing house is not a person's name, consult the *MLA Handbook for Writers of Research Papers,* use an abbreviation of your own that clearly identifies the publisher, or give the publisher's name in full, except for the kinds of words and abbreviations described above.

Abrams	Harry N. Abrams, Inc.	ALA	American Library Association
Allyn	Allyn and Bacon, Inc.	Appleton	Appleton-Century-Crofts
Ballantine	Ballantine Books, Inc.	Bantam	Bantam Books, Inc.
Barnes	Barnes and Noble Books	Basic	Basic Books

Bobbs	The Bobbs-Merrill Co., Inc.	Clarendon	Clarendon Press
Dell	Dell Publishing Co., Inc.	Dodd	Dodd, Mead and Co.
Doubleday	Doubleday and Co., Inc.	Dover	Dover Publications, Inc.
Dutton	E. P. Dutton, Inc.	Funk	Funk and Wagnalls, Inc.
GPO	Government Printing Office	Harcourt	Harcourt Brace Jovanovich, Inc.
Harper	Harper and Row, Publishers, Inc., HarperCollins Publishers, Inc.	Holt	Holt, Rinehart, and Winston, Inc.
Houghton	Houghton Mifflin Co.	Knopf	Alfred A. Knopf, Inc.
Lippincott	J. B. Lippincott Co.	Little	Little, Brown and Co.
McDougal	McDougal Littell Inc.	McGraw	McGraw-Hill, Inc.
Macmillan	Macmillan Publishing Co., Inc.	MLA	The Modern Language Association of America
Norton	W. W. Norton and Co., Inc.	Penguin	Penguin Books, Inc.
Pocket	Pocket Books	Prentice	Prentice-Hall, Inc.
Putnam's	G. P. Putnam's Sons	Rand	Rand McNally and Co.
Random	Random House, Inc.	St. Martin's	St. Martin's Press, Inc.
Scott	Scott, Foresman and Co.	Simon	Simon and Schuster, Inc.
Twayne	Twayne Publishers	Viking	The Viking Press, Inc.

Sacred Works and Literary Works

For abbreviations of parts of the Bible and other scriptures, consult a dictionary. For standard abbreviations of works by Shakespeare and other classic works of literature, see the *MLA Handbook for Writers of Research Papers.*

Other Abbreviations for Use in Documentation

The following abbreviations, in addition to the ones given on the preceding pages, are commonly used in documentation.

abr.	abridged	ch.	chapter
chs.	chapters	col.	column

cols.	columns	comp.	compiled by, compiler
cond.	conducted by, conductor	dir.	directed by, director
ed.	edited by, editor, edition	eds.	editors, editions
et al.	*et alii, et aliae* ("and others")	fig.	figure
fwd.	foreword, foreword by	illus.	illustrated by, illustrator, illustration
introd.	introduced by, introduction	n.d.	no date
no.	number	n.p.	no place, no publisher
P	Press	p.	page
par.	paragraph	pp.	pages
qtd.	quoted	rev.	revised by, revision, review
rpt.	reprinted by, reprint	sc.	scene
sec.	section	ser.	series
trans.	translated by, translator, translation	U	University
vers.	version	vol.	volume
vols.	volumes	writ.	written by, writer

Forms for Working Bibliography and Works Cited Entries

The following are some basic forms for bibliographic entries. Use these forms on the bibliography cards that make up your working bibliography and in the Works Cited list that appears at the end of your paper.

Whole Books

The following models can also be used for reports and pamphlets.

A. One author

> Ruiz, Ramón Eduardo. <u>Triumphs and Tragedy: A History of the Mexican People</u>. New York: Norton, 1992.

B. Two authors

> Gilbert, Sandra M., and Susan Gubar. <u>The Madwoman in the Attic: The Woman Writer and the Nineteenth-Century Literary Imagination</u>. New Haven: Yale UP, 1979.

C. Three authors

> Demko, George J., Jerome Agel, and Eugene Boe. <u>Why in the World: Adventures in Geography</u>. New York: Anchor-Doubleday, 1992.

D. Four or more authors

The abbreviation *et al.* means "and others." Use *et al.* instead of listing all the editors.

> Gatto, Joseph, et al. <u>Exploring Visual Design</u>. 2nd ed. Worcester: Davis, 1987.

E. No author identified

Literary Market Place: The Directory of the American
        Book Publishing Industry. 1997 ed. New York:
        Bowker, 1996.

F. An editor, but no single author

Nabokov, Peter, ed. Native American Testimony: A
        Chronicle of Indian-White Relations from Prophecy
        to the Present, 1492-1992. New York: Viking-
        Penguin, 1991.

G. Two or three editors

Pryor, Karen, and Kenneth S. Norris, eds. Dolphin
        Societies: Discoveries and Puzzles. Berkeley: U of
        California P, 1991.

H. Four or more editors

The abbreviation *et al.* means "and others." Use *et al.* instead of listing all the editors.

McFarlan, Donald, et al., eds. The Guinness Book of
        Records 1992. New York: Facts on File, 1991.

I. An author and a translator

Soseki, Natsume. Kokoro: A Novel and Selected Essays.
        Trans. Edwin McClellan and Jay Rubin. New York:
        Madison, 1992.

J. An author, a translator, and an editor

Capellanus, Andreas. The Art of Courtly Love. Abr. ed.
        Trans. John J. Parry. Ed. Frederick W. Locke. New
        York: Ungar, 1976.

K. An edition other than the first

Janson, H. W., and Anthony F. Janson. History of Art
        for Young People. 4th ed. New York: Abrams, 1992.

L. A book or monograph that is part of a series

```
LaRusso, Carol Spenard, comp. The Green Thoreau.
     Classic Wisdom Ser. San Rafael: New World, 1992.
```

M. A multivolume work

If you have used only one volume of a multivolume work, cite only that volume.

```
Child, Francis James, ed. The English and Scottish
     Popular Ballads. 1883-98. Vol 1. New York: Dover,
     1965. 2 vols.
```

If you have used more than one volume of a multivolume work, cite the entire work.

```
Child, Francis James, ed. The English and Scottish
     Popular Ballads. 1883-98. 2 vols. New York: Dover,
     1965.
```

N. A volume with its own title that is part of a multivolume work with a different title

```
Durant, Will, and Ariel Durant. Rousseau and
     Revolution: A History of Civilization in France,
     England, and Germany from 1756, and in the
     Remainder of Europe from 1715, to 1789. New York:
     Simon, 1967. Vol. 10 of The Story of Civilization.
     11 vols. 1935-75.
```

O. A republished book or a literary work available in several editions

Give the date of the original publication after the title. Then give complete publication information, including the date, for the edition that you have used.

```
Steinbeck, John. The Grapes of Wrath. 1939. New York:
     Penguin, 1999.
```

P. A government publication

Give the name of the government (country or state). Then give the department, followed by the agency if applicable. Next give the title, followed by the author if known. Then give the publication information. The publisher of U.S. government documents is usually the Government Printing Office, or GPO.

```
United States. Dept. of Education. Office of
     Educational Research and Improvement.
     OERI Publications Guide. By Lance
     Ferderer.  Washington: GPO, 1990.

---. ---. ---. Educational Resources Information
     Center. Recent Department of Education
     Publications in ERIC. Washington: GPO, 1992.
```

Parts of Books

A.   A poem, short story, essay, or chapter in a collection of works by one author

```
Cather, Willa. "Joseph and His Brothers." Cather:
     Stories, Poems, and Other Writings. Comp. Sharon
     O'Brien. New York: Viking, 1992. 859-71.
```

B.   A poem, short story, essay, or chapter in a collection of works by several authors

```
West, Paul. "Pelé."  The Norton Book of Sports. Ed.
     George Plimpton. New York: Norton, 1992. 308.
```

C.   A novel or play in an anthology

```
Simmons, Alexander. Sherlock Holmes and the Hands of
     Othello. Black Thunder: An Anthology of
     Contemporary African American Drama. Ed. William
     B. Branch. New York: Mentor, 1992. 359-415.
```

D.   An introduction, preface, foreword, or afterword written by the author(s) of a work

```
Pinson, Linda, and Jerry Jinnett. Dedication. The Woman
     Entrepreneur. Ed. Pinson and Jinnett. Tustin: Out
     of Your Mind, 1992. iii.
```

E. An introduction, preface, foreword, or afterword written by someone other than the author(s) of a work

```
Coles, Robert. Foreword. No Place to Be: Voices of
     Homeless Children. By Judith Berck. Boston:
     Houghton, 1992. 1-4.
```

F. Cross-references

If you have used more than one work from a collection, you may give a complete entry for the collection. Then, in the separate entries for the works, you can refer to the entry for the whole collection by using the editor's last name or, if you have listed more than one work by that editor, the editor's last name and a shortened version of the title.

```
French, Warren, ed. A Companion to The Grapes of Wrath.
     New York: Viking, 1963.

---. "What Did John Steinbeck Know About the 'Okies'?"
     French, Companion 51-53.

Steinbeck, John. Their Blood Is Strong. San Francisco:
     Lubin, 1938. Rpt. in French, Companion 53-92.
```

G. A reprinted article or essay (one previously published elsewhere)

If a work that appears in a collection first appeared in another place, give complete information for the original publication, followed by *Rpt. in* and complete information for the collection.

```
Searle, John. "What Is a Speech Act?" Philosophy in
     America. Ed. Max Black. London: Allen, 1965. 221-
     39. Rpt. in Readings in the Philosophy of
     Language. Ed. Jay F. Rosenberg and Charles Travis.
     Englewood Cliffs: Prentice, 1971. 614-28.
```

Magazines, Journals, Newspapers, and Encyclopedias

A. An article in a magazine, journal, or newspaper

```
Smith, Shelley. "Baseball's Forgotten Pioneers." Sports
     Illustrated 30 Mar. 1992: 72.

Schwartz, Felice N. "Women as a Business Imperative."
     Harvard Business Review 70.2 (1992): 105—13.

"Kozyrev's Mission to Washington." Editorial. Boston
     Globe 14 June 1992: 78.
```

If no author is identified, begin with the article's title. If an author is identified, begin with the author's name followed by the article's title. When an article continues on a page that does not immediately follow its first page, use a plus sign (+) after the number of the page on which it begins.

B. An article in an encyclopedia or other alphabetically organized reference work

Give the title of the article, the name of the reference work, and the year of the edition.

```
"Zuni." Encyclopaedia Britannica: Micropaedia. 1992 ed.
```

C. A review

```
Kellow, Brian. Rev. of Don Pasquale. Metropolitan Opera
     Guild Education Department. Columbia U Kathryn
     Bache Miller Theater, New York. Opera News June
     1992: 52.
```

If the review is unsigned, begin with *Rev. of* and the title.

Media and Other Sources

A. An interview that you have conducted or letter you have received

```
Jackson, Jesse. Personal interview [or Letter to the
    author]. 15 July 1992.
```

B. A film

```
The Grapes of Wrath. Screenplay by Nunnally Johnson.
    Dir. John Ford. Perf. John Carradine, Jane
    Darwell, and Henry Fonda. Twentieth Century-Fox,
    1940.
```

C. A work of art (painting, photography, sculpture)

```
Catlin, George. Four Bears, Second Chief, in Full
    Dress. National Museum of American Art,
    Smithsonian Institution, Washington.
```

D. A television or radio program

Give the episode name (if applicable) and the series or program name. Include any information that you have about the program's writer and director. Then give the network, the local station, the city, and the date the program aired.

```
"A Desert Blooming." Living Wild. Writ. Marshall
    Riggan. Dir. Harry L. Gorden. PBS. WTTW, Chicago.
    29 Apr. 1984.
```

E. A musical composition

```
Chopin, Frédéric. Waltz in A-flat major, op. 42.
```

F. A sound recording (compact disc, LP, or audiocassette)

If the recording is not a compact disc, include *LP* or *Audiocassette* before the manufacturer's name.

```
Guthrie, Woody. "Do-Re-Me." Dust Bowl Ballads. Rounder,
    1988.
```

G. A lecture, speech, or address

Give the name of the speaker followed by the title of the speech (if applicable), or the kind of speech (*Lecture, Introduction, Address*). Then give the event, the place, and the date.

```
Benjamin, John. Address. First Annual Abolitionist
     March and Rally. Boston. 18 July 1992.
```

Electronic Media

Because the number of electronic information sources is great and increasing rapidly, please refer to the most current edition of the MLA Handbook for Writers of Research Papers *if you need more complete information. You can also refer to the page "MLA Style" on the Modern Language Association Web site <http://www.mla.org/>.*

Portable databases (CD-ROM, DVDs, laser discs, diskettes, and videocassettes)

These products contain fixed information (information that cannot be changed unless a new version is produced and released). Citing them in a research paper is similar to citing printed sources. You should include the following information:

- Name of the author (if applicable)
- Title of the part of the work used (if applicable), underlined or in quotation marks
- Title of the product or database (underlined)
- Publication medium (CD-ROM, DVD, laser disc, diskette, or videocassette)
- Edition, release, or version (if applicable)
- City of publication
- Name of publisher
- Year of publication

If you cannot find some of this information, cite what is available.

```
Boyer, Paul S., et al. "Troubled Agriculture." The
     Enduring Vision: A History of the American People.
     Interactive Edition. CD-ROM. Vers. 1.1. Lexington:
     Heath, 1993.

"Steinbeck's Dust Bowl Saga." Our Times Multimedia
     Encyclopedia of the 20th Century. CD-ROM. 1996 ed.
     Redwood City: Vicarious, 1995.

"The Dust Bowl." In Perspective: Literary Themes in the
     Real World. Laser disc. McDougal, 1995.

Eyes on the Prize: America's Civil Rights Years. Prod.
     Blackside. 6 episodes. Videocassettes. PBS Video,
     1986.
```

Online Sources

Sources on the World Wide Web are numerous and include scholarly projects, reference databases, articles in periodicals, and professional and personal sites. Not all sites are equally reliable, and therefore material gathered from the World Wide Web should be evaluated carefully. Entries for online sources in the Works Cited list should contain as much of the information listed below as is available.

- Name of the author, editor, compiler, or translator, accompanied by an abbreviation, such as *ed., comp.,* or *trans.,* if applicable

- Title of the material. Use quotation marks for poems, short stories, articles, and similar short works. Underline the title of a book.

- Publication information for any print version of the source

- Title (underlined) of the scholarly project, database, periodical, or professional or personal site. For a professional or personal site with no title, add a description such as *Home page* (neither underlined nor in quotation marks).

- Name of the editor of the scholarly project or database

- For a journal, the volume number, issue number, or other identifying number

- Date of electronic publication, of the latest update, or of posting

- For a work from a subscription service, the name of the service and—if a library is the subscriber—the name of the library and the town or state where it is located.

- Range or total number of pages, paragraphs, or other sections if they are numbered

- Name of any institution or organization that sponsors or is associated with the Web site

- Date the source was accessed

- Electronic address, or URL, of the source. For a subscription service, use the URL of the service's main page (if known) or the keyword assigned to the service.

Scholarly project

> <u>Martha Heasley Cox Center for Steinbeck Studies</u>. Sept. 1999. San Jose State U. 30 Sept. 1999 <http://www.sjsu.edu/depts/steinbec/srchome.html>.

Professional site

> <u>American Council of Learned Societies Home Page</u>. 1998. Amer. Council of Learned Societies. 30 Sept. 1999 <http://www.acls.org/jshome.htm>.

Personal site

> Stephan, Ed. <u>John Steinbeck: The California Novels</u>. 30
>   Sept. 1999 <http://www.ac.wwu.edu/~stephan/
>   Steinbeck/index.html>.

Book

> Mabbutt, J. A., and Andrew W. Wilson, eds. <u>Social and
>   Environmental Aspects of Desertification</u>. Tokyo:
>   United Nations UP, 1980. 20 Jan. 2000
>   <http://www.unu.edu/unupress/unupbooks/80127e/
>   80127E00.htm>.

Article in reference database

> "Dust Bowl." <u>Encyclopaedia Britannica Online</u>. Vers.
>   99.1. Encyclopaedia Britannica. 1 Oct. 1999
>   <http://www.eb.com:180/bol/topic?eu=32140&sctn=1>.

Article in journal

> Park, Tai H. "Morality, Individual Responsibility, and
>   the Law." <u>Philosophy and Literature</u> 22.1 (1998).
>   6 Oct. 1999 <http://www.press.jhu.edu/journals/
>   philosophy_and_literature/v022/22.1park.html>.

Article in magazine

> Chiles, James R. "Bang! Went the Doors of Every Bank in
>   America." <u>Smithsonian</u> Apr 1997. Abstract. 1 Oct.
>   1999 <http://www.smithsonianmag.si.edu/
>   smithsonian/issues97/apr97/banks.html>.

Work from subscription service

> "Dust Bowl." <u>Compton's Encyclopedia Online</u>. Vers. 3.0.
>   1998. America Online. 5 Oct. 1999. Keyword:
>   Compton's.

> Hinton, Rebecca. "Steinbeck's <u>The Grapes of Wrath</u>."
>   <u>Explicator</u> 56 (Winter 1998): 101—03. <u>WilsonSelect</u>.
>   FirstSearch. Evanston Public Lib., IL. 4 Oct. 1999
>   <http://firstsearch.oclc.org.

Alternative Documentation Styles

The documentation style suggested in this book, which involves parenthetical citations and a Works Cited list, is recommended in the *MLA Handbook for Writers of Research Papers* and is widely used for work in languages, literature, the arts, and the humanities throughout the English-speaking world. However, other approaches to documentation are possible. One common approach is to use endnotes or footnotes.

Endnote and Footnote Styles

Some people prefer endnotes or footnotes to parenthetical citations because they do not clutter the text of the research paper. Instead of a citation, what appears in the text is a number placed after a sentence and above the line, as in the following example:

```
Colonel Shaw's mother is said to have cried from

happiness on seeing her son at the head of the all-

African-American 54th Massachusetts.5
```

The number that is placed above the line is called a **superscript.** Throughout the paper, information taken from sources is marked with such superscripts. Each superscript refers the reader to a note that appears either at the bottom of that page or at the end of the paper. If the note appears at the bottom of the page, it is called a **footnote.** If it appears at the end of the paper, it is called an **endnote.** Footnotes have become unpopular in recent years because of their tendency to clutter the pages of a paper. Most writers who use notes instead of parenthetical citations prefer endnotes. The following is a sample endnote or footnote:

⁵ Shelby Foote, <u>Fredericksburg to Meridian</u> (New York: Random, 1963), vol. 2 of <u>The Civil War: A Narrative</u>, 3 vols. (1958–74) 697.

An endnote or footnote differs from a Working Bibliography or Works Cited entry in the following ways:

1. The first line of a working bibliography or Works Cited entry begins at the left margin. The first line of an endnote or footnote is indented five spaces.

2. Run-over lines of a working bibliography or Works Cited entry are indented five spaces. Run-over lines of an endnote or footnote begin at the left margin.

3. A working bibliography or Works Cited entry does not have a superscript at the beginning. An endnote or footnote does.

4. The name at the beginning of a working bibliography or Works Cited entry is reversed for alphabetizing. In an endnote or footnote, the name is given in its normal order.

5. A working bibliography or Works Cited entry has three main parts, each of which ends with a period: the name, the title, and the publication information. An endnote or footnote has four main parts, only the last of which ends with a period: the name, the title, the publication information, and the page number(s).

6. The publication information in an endnote or footnote is enclosed in parentheses. In a working bibliography or Works Cited entry, it is not.

For proper placement of endnotes and footnotes, see the samples on pages 110–112. The following pages give sample forms for endnotes and footnotes.

Sample Forms for Endnotes or Footnotes

Whole Books

The following models can also be used for reports and pamphlets.

A. One author

1 Ramón Eduardo Ruiz, <u>Triumphs and Tragedy: A History of the Mexican People</u> (New York: Norton, 1992) 14.

B. Two authors

2 Sandra M. Gilbert and Susan Gubar, <u>The Madwoman in the Attic: The Woman Writer and the Nineteenth-Century Literary Imagination</u> (New Haven: Yale UP, 1979) 65.

C. Three authors

3 George J. Demko, Jerome Agel, and Eugene Boe, <u>Why in the World: Adventures in Geography</u> (New York: Anchor-Doubleday, 1992) 15-16.

D. Four or more authors

The abbreviation *et al.* means "and others." Use *et al.* instead of listing all the authors.

4 Joseph Gatto, et al., <u>Exploring Visual Design</u>, 2nd ed. (Worcester: Davis, 1987) 43.

E. No author identified

5 <u>Literary Market Place: The Directory of the American Book Publishing Industry</u>, 1997 ed. (New York: Bowker, 1996) 1673.

F. An editor, but no single author

6 Peter Nabokov, ed., <u>Native American Testimony: A Chronicle of Indian-White Relations from Prophecy to the Present, 1492-1992</u> (New York: Viking-Penguin, 1991) 101.

G. Two or three editors

7 Karen Pryor and Kenneth S. Norris, eds., <u>Dolphin</u>

<u>Societies: Discoveries and Puzzles</u> (Berkeley: U of California P, 1991) 36.

H. Four or more editors

The abbreviation *et al.* means "and others." Use *et al.* instead of listing all the editors.

[8] Donald McFarlan, et al., eds., <u>The Guinness Book of Records 1992</u> (New York: Facts on File, 1991) 99.

I. An author and a translator

[9] Natsume Soseki, <u>Kokoro: A Novel and Selected Essays</u>, trans. Edwin McClellan and Jay Rubin (New York: Madison, 1992) 115.

J. An author, a translator, and an editor

[10] Andreas Capellanus, <u>The Art of Courtly Love</u>, abr. ed., trans. John J. Parry, ed. Frederick W. Locke (New York: Ungar, 1976) 42.

K. An edition other than the first

[11] H. W. Janson and Anthony F. Janson, <u>History of Art for Young People</u>, 4th ed. (New York: Abrams, 1992) 45.

L. A book or monograph that is part of a series

[12] Carol Spenard LaRusso, comp., <u>The Green Thoreau</u>, Classic Wisdom Ser. (San Rafael: New World, 1992) 47.

M. A multivolume work

If you are referring to a particular place in one volume, use this form:

[13] Francis James Child, ed., <u>The English and Scottish Popular Ballads</u>, vol. 1 (1883-98; New York: Dover, 1965) 22.

Endnotes and footnotes that refer to entire works are quite rare. However, if you are referring to an entire multivolume work, use the following form, with no page number:

[14] Francis James Child, ed., <u>The English and Scottish Popular Ballads</u>, 2 vols. (1883-98; New York: Dover, 1965).

N. A volume with its own title that is part of a multivolume work with a different title

15 Will Durant and Ariel Durant, <u>Rousseau and Revolution: A History of Civilization in France, England, and Germany from 1756, and in the Rest of Europe from 1715, to 1789</u> (New York: Simon, 1967), vol. 10 of <u>The Story of Civilization</u>, 11 vols (1935-75) 18.

O. A republished book or a literary work available in several editions

Give the date of the orginal publication, followed by a semicolon, then give the place of publication and the date of the edition that you have used.

16 John Steinbeck, <u>The Grapes of Wrath</u> (1939; New York: Penguin, 1999) 339.

P. A government publication

Give the name of the government (country or state). Then give the department, followed by the agency if applicable. Next give the title, followed by the author if known. Then give the publication information. The publisher of U.S. government documents is usually the Government Printing Office, or GPO.

17 United States, Dept. of Education, Office of Educational Research and Improvement, <u>OERI Publications Guide</u>, by Lance Ferderer (Washington: GPO, 1990) 27.

18 ---, ---, ---, Educational Resources Information Center, <u>Recent Department of Education Publications in ERIC</u> (Washington: GPO, 1992) 162.

Parts of Books

A. A poem, short story, essay, or chapter in a collection of works by one author

19 Willa Cather, "Joseph and His Brothers," <u>Cather: Stories, Poems, and Other Writings</u>, comp. Sharon O'Brien (New York: Viking, 1992) 860.

B. A poem, short story, essay, or chapter in a collection of works by several authors

   [20] Paul West, "Pelé," <u>The Norton Book of Sports</u>, ed. George Plimpton (New York: Norton, 1992) 308.

C. A novel or play in an anthology

   [21] Alexander Simmons, <u>Sherlock Holmes and the Hands of Othello</u>, <u>Black Thunder: An Anthology of Contemporary African American Drama</u>, ed. William B. Branch (New York: Mentor, 1992) 411.

D. An introduction, preface, foreword, or afterword written by the author(s) of a work

   [22] Linda Pinson and Jerry Jinnett, dedication, <u>The Woman Entrepreneur</u>, ed. Pinson and Jinnett (Tustin: Out of Your Mind, 1992) iii.

E. An introduction, preface, foreword, or afterword written by someone other than the author(s) of a work

   [23] Robert Coles, foreword, <u>No Place to Be: Voices of Homeless Children</u>, by Judith Berck (Boston: Houghton, 1992) 2.

F. A reprinted article or essay (one previously published elsewhere)

If a work that appears in a collection first appeared in another place, give complete information for the original publication, followed by *rpt. in* and complete information for the collection.

   [24] John Searle, "What Is a Speech Act?" <u>Philosophy in America</u>, ed. Max Black (London: Allen, 1965) 221-39, rpt. in <u>Readings in the Philosophy of Language</u>, ed. Jay F. Rosenberg and Charles Travis (Englewood Cliffs: Prentice, 1971) 615.

Magazines, Journals, Newspapers, Encyclopedias, and Newsletters

A. An article in a magazine, journal, or newspaper

25 Shelley Smith, "Baseball's Forgotten Pioneers," <u>Sports Illustrated</u> 30 Mar. 1992: 72.

26 Felice N. Schwartz, "Women as a Business Imperative," <u>Harvard Business Review</u> 70.2 (1992): 105—13.

27 "Kozyrev's Mission to Washington," editorial, <u>Boston Globe</u> 14 June 1992: 78.

If no author is identified, begin with the articles title. If an author is identified, begin with the author's name followed by the article's title. When an article continues on a page that does not immediately follow its first page, use a plus sign (+) after the number of the page on which it begins.

B. An article in an encyclopedia or other alphabetically organized reference work

Give the title of the article, the name of the reference work, and the year of the edition.

28 "Zuni," <u>Encyclopaedia Britannica: Micropaedia</u>, 1992 ed.

C. A review

29 Brian Kellow, rev. of <u>Don Pasquale</u>, Metropolitan Opera Guild Education Department, Kathryn Bache Miller Theater, New York, <u>Opera News</u> June 1992: 52.

If the review is unsigned, begin with *Rev. of* and the title.

Media and Other Sources

A. An interview you have conducted or letter you have received

31 Jesse Jackson, personal interview [or letter to the author], 15 July 1992.

B. A film

32 <u>The Grapes of Wrath</u>, screenplay by Nunnally Johnson, dir. John Ford, perf. John Carradine, Jane Darwell, and Henry Fonda, Twentieth Century-Fox, 1940.

C. A work of art (painting, photograph, sculpture)

33 George Catlin, <u>Four Bears, Second Chief, in Full Dress</u>, National Museum of American Art, Smithsonian Institution, Washington.

D. A television or radio program

Give the episode name (if applicable) and the series or program name. Include any information that you have about the program's writer and director. Then give the network, the local station, the city, and the date the program aired.

34 "A Desert Blooming," <u>Living Wild</u>, writ. Marshall Riggan, dir. Harry L. Gorden, PBS, WTTW, Chicago, 29 Apr. 1984.

E. A musical composition

35 Frédéric Chopin, Waltz in A-flat major, op. 42.

F. A sound recording (compact disc, LP, or audiocassette)

If the recording is not a compact disc, include *LP* or *audiocassette* before the manufacturer's name.

36 Woody Guthrie, "Do-Re-Me," <u>Dust Bowl Ballads</u>, Rounder, 1988.

G. A lecture, speech, or address

Give the name of the speaker followed by the title of the speech (if applicable) or the kind of speech *(lecture, introduction, address)*. Then give the event, the place, and the date.

37 John Benjamin, address, First Annual Abolitionist March and Rally, Boston, 18 July 1992.

Electronic Media

Because the number of electronic information sources is great and increasing rapidly, please refer to the most current edition of the MLA Handbook for Writers of Research Papers *if you need more complete information.*

Portable databases (CD-ROM, DVDs, videodiscs, diskettes, and videocassettes)

These products contain fixed information (information that cannot be changed unless a new version is produced and released). Citing them in a research paper is similar to citing printed sources. You should include the following information:

- Name of the author (if applicable)
- Title of the part of the work used (if applicable) underlined or in quotation marks
- Title of the product or database (underlined)
- Publication medium (CD-ROM, DVD, laser disc, diskette, or videocassette)
- Edition, release, or version (if applicable)
- City of publication
- Name of publisher
- Year of publication

If you cannot find some of this information, cite what is available.

[38] Paul S. Boyer, et al, "Troubled Agriculture," <u>The Enduring Vision: A History of the American People, Interactive Edition</u>, CD-ROM, vers. 1.1 (Lexington: Heath, 1993).

[39] "Steinbeck's Dust Bowl Saga," <u>Our Times Multimedia Encyclopedia of the 20th Century</u>, CD-ROM, 1996 ed. (Redwood City: Vicarious, 1995).

[40] "The Dust Bowl." <u>In Perspective: Literary Themes in the Real World</u>, laser disc, McDougal, 1995.

[41] <u>Eyes on the Prize: America's Civil Rights Years,</u> prod. Blackside, 6 episodes, videocassettes, PBS Video, 1986.

Online Sources

Because online resources may be updated or changed frequently, it is important to include complete information when citing them:

- Name of the author, editor, compiler, or translator, accompanied by an abbreviation, such as *ed., comp.,* or *trans.,* if applicable

- Title of the material, underlined or enclosed in quotation marks as necessary.

- Publication information for any print version of the source

- Title of the Web site, underlined

- Name of the editor of the scholarly project or database

- For a journal, the volume number, issue number, or other identifying number

- Date of electronic publication, latest update, or posting

- For a work from a subscription service, the name of the service and—if a library is the subscriber—the name of the library and the town or state where it is located.

- Range or number of pages, paragraphs, or other sections

- Name of any institution or organization associated with the Web site

- Date the source was accessed

- Electronic address, or URL, of the source. For a subscription service, use the URL of the service's main page (if known) or the keyword assigned to the service.

42 <u>Martha Heasley Cox Center for Steinbeck Studies</u>, Sept. 1999, San Jose State U, 30 Sept. 1999 <http://www.sjsu.edu/depts/steinbec/srchome.html>.

43 J. A. Mabbutt and Andrew W. Wilson, eds., <u>Social and Environmental Aspects of Desertification</u> (Tokyo: United Nations UP, 1980), 20 Jan. 2000 <http://www.unu.edu/ unupress/unupbooks/80127e/80127E00.htm>.

44 James R. Chiles, "Bang! Went the Doors of Every Bank in America," <u>Smithsonian</u> Apr. 1997, abstract, 1 Oct 1999 <http://www.smithsonianmag.si.edu/smithsonian/issues97/ apr97/banks.html>.

45 "Dust Bowl," <u>Compton's Encyclopedia Online</u>, vers. 3.0, 1998, America Online, 5 Oct. 1999, keyword: Compton's.

For additional information on citing online sources, see pages 90–91.

Subsequent References

The first time that you write an endnote or footnote for a work, give a full entry. Thereafter, you can give the author's or editor's name by itself.

[51] Warren French, "What Did John Steinbeck Know About the 'Okies'?" <u>A Companion to</u> The Grapes of Wrath, ed. French (New York: Viking, 1963) 52.

[52] French 53.

If you have cited more than one work by the author or editor, then include shortened forms of the titles in subsequent endnotes or footnotes.

[53] French, "What Did" 53.

Other Types of Documentation

Two other documentation styles are in widespread use today. The **author-date system** is used widely in the sciences. This system is similar to parenthetical documentation, but each paranthetical citation includes the date of publication and the page number(s), preceded by *p.* or *pp.*, after the author's or editor's last name.

```
Colonel Shaw's mother is said to have cried from

happiness on seeing her son at the head of the all-

African-American 54th Massachusetts (Foote,

1958-74,Vol. 2, p.697).
```

As the following example shows, the Works Cited entries used in the author-date system differ in a number of ways from those used in the parenthetical-documentation system. For details about the preparation of such entries, see the *Publication Manual of the American Psychological Association*.

```
Foote, S. (1958-74). The Civil War: A Narrative.

    (Vols. 1-3). New York: Random House.
```

If the Works Cited list contains more than one work published by the same author or editor in the same year, then lowercase letters (*a, b, c,* and so on) are used to distinguish the works.

> The Okies expected to find a paradise in California,
> but what they found instead when they reached the end
> of their journey was "a man-blighted Eden" (Crockett,
> 1962a, p. 195).

Crockett, H. (1962a). The Bible and <u>The grapes of wrath</u>.
<u>College English,</u> <u>24</u>, 193-99.

In the **number system** of documentation, each entry in the Works Cited list is numbered with an Arabic numeral (1, 2, 3, and so on). The entries are usually arranged in the order in which the works are cited in the research paper. Here are two examples of such entries.

1. Burchard, P. <u>One gallant rush: Robert Could Shaw and
   his brave black regiment</u>. New York: St. Martin's Press,
   1965.

2. Foote, S. <u>The Civil War: A narrative</u>. 3 vols. New York:
   Random House, 1958-74.

A parenthetical citation in the text of the research paper consists of the number of a Works Cited entry, a comma, the abbreviation *p.* or *pp.*, and the page number(s).

> Colonel Shaw's mother is said to have cried from

```
happiness on seeing her son at the head of the all-

African-American 54th Massachusetts (2, Vol. 2,

p. 697).
```

Other Style Manuals

The documentation style used in this book is that of the *MLA Handbook for Writers of Research Papers.* Other styles are often followed in the sciences. Here is a list of style manuals commonly used by people doing scientific and mathematical research in the United States:

The ACS Style Guide: A Manual for Authors and Editors

AMS Handbook

Publication Manual of the American Psychological Association

Scientific Style and Format: The CBE Manual for Authors, Editors, and Publishers

Suggestions to Authors of the Reports of the United States Geological Survey

Another style manual that is widely used in a variety of fields, especially in the humanities, is *The Chicago Manual of Style.*

Marcus Washington

Mr. Zacharis

American History

3 May 1993

The "Victory" of the Massachusetts 54th

at Fort Wagner

On Boston Common, near the Massachusetts State House, stands
an impressive monument--a sculpture depicting a group of African-
American soldiers marching in the uniforms of the Union Army.[1] This
monument commemorates the brave men of the Massachusetts 54th
Infantry Regiment, who on July 18, 1863, at the height of the Civil
War, stormed a South Carolina earthwork known as Fort Wagner or
Battery Wagner. When the fighting was done, nearly half of those men
lay dead in what was by all accounts a massacre, an overwhelming
victory for the Confederacy.[2] However, the events at Fort Wagner
were strangely contradictory. Although many Yankee soldiers lost
their lives in the charge, and although the Confederates
technically won the battle, one can rightly claim that the battle
was a great victory for the Union Army and for all people of color.

The first calls for recruitment of African-American soldiers
into the Union Army came from abolitionist leaders. Frederick
Douglass, the charismatic African-American orator, newspaper
editor, and abolitionist, had proclaimed, "The arm of the slaves
[is] the best defense against the arm of the slaveholder. [. . .]
Who would be free themselves must strike the blow."[3] Wendell
Phillips, a leader of the Boston abolitionists, had declared, "We
have given the sword to the white man; the time has come to give it
to the black!"[4] According to historian Barbara Fields, a convention
of free African Americans meeting in 1863 resolved: "It is time now
for more effective remedies to be thoroughly tried in the shape of
warm lead and cold steel duly administered by 100,000 black
doctors."[5] By that time, Congress had authorized the enlistment of

This is a sample paper done in endnote style. For a sample page in footnote style, see page 112.

Note that numbers referring to endnotes are **superscripted,** or slightly raised above the line.

The brackets enclose a slight modification made to the source in order to fit it grammatically into the paper.

African-American troops, a move that met with the full support of
Ulysses S. Grant:

> I have given the subject of arming the Negro my hearty
> support. This, with the emancipation of the Negro, is
> the heaviest blow yet given the Confederacy. [. . .] We
> have added a powerful ally. They will make good soldiers
> and taking them from the enemy weakens him in the same
> proportion they strengthen us.[6]

The African-American 54th Massachusetts Infantry Regiment was
the brainchild of Governor John A. Andrew, who on January 26, 1863,
had responded to Lincoln's Emancipation Proclamation by writing to
Edwin Stanton, Lincoln's secretary of war, requesting permission to
raise a regiment of troops of African-American descent.[7] To lead
the regiment, Andrew chose a young soldier named Robert Gould Shaw,
from a staunchly antislavery family in Boston.[8] By May 14, one
thousand men had volunteered to serve in the 54th.[9] For some time,
however, the Union commanders were reluctant to put their African-
American troops into combat.[10] On July 6, Colonel Shaw wrote to
Brigadier General George C. Strong, complaining that his men were
not being put to use.[11] On July 18, Shaw and his regiment got their
chance to see action.

Fort Wagner, "perhaps the strongest [earthwork] ever built,"
sat on the Atlantic coast at the mouth of Charleston Harbor. Taking
Fort Wagner was part of the Union Army's overall plan to take the
city of Charleston.[12] Unfortunately for the Union troops, the only
approach to the fort was a narrow area less than two hundred yards
wide.[13] Any troops crossing that area would be in grave danger from
the Confederate troops stationed inside the fort. Colonel Shaw
enthusiastically agreed to lead the attack on Fort Wagner.[14] The
attack began at 7:30 at night:

> The 1000-man rebel garrison came out of the bombproof to
> which it had retired at the height of the cannonade and

Note that a superscript is placed outside a final quotation mark.

A long quotation is set off from the text and indented ten spaces. The superscript follows the end of the quotation.

106

met the attackers. [. . .] When flesh and blood could
stand no more, the survivors fell back from the ditch
and parapet, black and white alike, and returned to the
trenches they had left an hour ago. Casualties had been
heavy; 1515 of the attackers had fallen, as compared to
174 of the defenders. [. . .] Next morning [. . .] a
brief truce sufficed for removal of the wounded and
disposal of the slain, including the twenty-six-year-old
Shaw.[15]

It was a terrible defeat, and yet there are two reasons for
considering it a victory as well. The first reason is that the
charge of the men of the 54th helped to create an attitude both
within them and within many whites that would make it difficult for
any Americans of African descent to be made slaves again. The
second reason is that the charge proved the value of African-
American soldiers and led to their further participation in the
war.

The bravery of the 54th Massachusetts proved that African
Americans could be good soldiers. After the charge on Fort Wagner,
the numbers of African-American enlisted men grew. A total of
180,000 African-American soldiers served with the Union Army during
the last years of the war--a force equal to an astonishing 85
percent of the eligible male African-American population.[16]

The charge on Fort Wagner was also a powerful blow against
slavery. The institution of slavery depended on the ability of
people to believe that some human beings were inherently less
capable or less worthy than others. As Confederate general Howell
Cobb had put it, "If slaves seem good soldiers, then our whole
theory of slavery is wrong."[17] The men of the 54th were determined
to prove that the theory was wrong. As one member of the 54th is
reported to have said, "We want 'em to know that we went down
standing up."[18] By not flinching from their duty, by charging onward

107

against overwhelming odds, the men of the 54th demonstrated their
courage and the falsehood of the racist assumption of lesser worth
underlying slavery. General William Tecumseh Sherman of the Union
forces pointed out, after African-American soldiers took up arms,
"They [the South] can't get back their slaves. It is dead."[19] It
was the fulfillment of a prophecy that Frederick Douglass had made:

> Once let a black man get upon his person the brass
> letters, "U.S." [. . .] get an eagle on his buttons and
> a musket on his shoulder and bullets in his pocket, and
> there is no power on earth which can deny that he has
> earned the right to citizenship in the United States.[20]

The charge of the 54th is considered by many African Americans
today a critical point in history, a point when their ancestors
established their right to citizenship. Monica Fairbanks, director
of the Afro-American History Museum in Boston, quotes with approval
William Carney, a member of the Massachusetts 54th who was awarded
the Congressional Medal of Honor: "We [. . .] take up arms in
defense of a nation to which we belong."[21] State Senator Bill Orin
of Massachusetts considers celebration of the memory of the
Massachusetts 54th to be equivalent to "celebrating the diversity
of the United States of America."[22] John Benjamin of the National
Park Service speaks of the importance of having the world recognize
"the contribution of the 54th to the freedom of our people."[23]
Gloria Fox, a Massachusetts state representative, says, "The
struggle continues—that's what [remembering] the 54th means."[24]
Each of these leaders recognizes the charge of the 54th not as a
defeat but as a great moral victory--a victory pulled, as the
proverb has it, from the jaws of defeat. That the charge of the
Massachusetts 54th is today remembered in this way is a fulfillment
of a prediction made by Abraham Lincoln:

> When victory is won, there will be some black men
> who can remember that, with silent tongue and

clenched teeth and steady eye and well-poised
bayonet, they have helped mankind on to a great
consummation.[25]

Ending with a
quotation is one
effective way to
conclude a research
paper or report.

Notes

[1] Augustus Saint-Gaudens, <u>Monument to Robert Gould Shaw and His Regiment</u>, Boston Common, Boston.

[2] Geoffrey Ward, <u>The Civil War: An Illustrated History</u> (New York: Knopf, 1990) 248.

[3] "The Universe of Battle," <u>The Civil War</u>, writ. Geoffrey C. Ward and Rick Burns with Ken Burns, dir. Ken Burns, Florentine, 1989.

[4] Peter Burchard, <u>One Gallant Rush: Robert Gould Shaw and His Brave Black Regiment</u> (New York: St. Martin's, 1965) 43.

[5] Ward 246-47.

[6] Ward 247.

[7] Burchard 2.

[8] Burchard 71.

[9] Burchard 90.

[10] Ward 247.

[11] Burchard 117-18.

[12] Burchard 120-21.

[13] Shelby Foote, <u>Fredericksburg to Meridian</u> (New York: Random, 1963), vol. 2 of <u>The Civil War: A Narrative</u>, 3 vols. (1958-74) 697.

[14] Burchard 133.

[15] Foote 697.

[16] "Universe."

[17] Qtd. in Ward 253.

[18] <u>Glory</u>, screenplay by Kevin Jarre, dir. Edward Zwick, perf. Matthew Broderick, Morgan Freeman, and Denzel Washington, Tri-Star, 1989.

[19] Qtd. in "Universe."

[20] Qtd. in Ward 246.

[21] Monica Fairbanks, personal interview, 18 July 1992.

[22] Bill Orin, address, First Annual Abolitionist March and Rally, Boston, 18 July 1992.

[23] John Benjamin, address, First Annual Abolitionist March and Rally, Boston, 18 July 1992.

[24] Gloria Fox, greeting, Abolitionist Rally at the African Meeting House, Boston, 18 July 1992.

[25] Qtd. in "Universe."

Marcus Washington

Mr. Zacharis

American History

3 May 1993

The "Victory" of the Massachusetts 54th

at Fort Wagner

On Boston Common, near the Massachusetts State House, stands an impressive monument--a sculpture depicting a group of African-American soldiers marching in the uniforms of the Union Army.[1] This monument commemorates the brave men of the Massachusetts 54th Infantry Regiment, who on July 18, 1863, at the height of the Civil War, stormed a South Carolina earthwork known as Fort Wagner or Battery Wagner. When the fighting was done, nearly half of those men lay dead in what was by all accounts a massacre, an overwhelming victory for the Confederacy.[2] However, the events at Fort Wagner were strangely contradictory. Although many Yankee soldiers lost their lives in the charge, and although the Confederates technically won the battle, one can rightly claim that the battle was a great victory for the Union Army and for all people of color.

The first calls for recruitment of African-American soldiers into the Union Army came from abolitionist leaders. Frederick Douglass, the charismatic African-American orator, newspaper editor, and abolitionist, had proclaimed, "The arm of the slaves [is] the best defense against the arm of the slaveholder. [. . .] Who would be free themselves must strike the blow."

---

[1] Augustus Saint-Gaudens, <u>Monument to Robert Gould Shaw and His Regiment</u>, Boston Common, Boston.

[2] Geoffrey Ward, <u>The Civil War: An Illustrated History</u> (New York: Knopf, 1990) 248.

Index